Spindrift is the spray blown off the crests of waves in winds of gale force and above. For sailors in a small boat, spindrift is the sign that forceful but workable conditions are becoming dangerous.

Spindrift

A Wilderness Pilgrimage at Sea

Peter Reason

 Vala

First published in 2014 by Vala Publishing Co-operative

Copyright © Peter Reason

Vala Publishing Co-operative Ltd

8 Gladstone Street, Bristol, BS3 3AY, UK

For further information on Vala publications, see

www.valapublishers.coop or write to info@valapublishers.coop

Illustrations, design and layout by Sue Gent

www.lupercaliadesign.com

Typeset in Freya, designed by Saku Heinänen

Printed and bound by CPI Group (UK) Ltd, Croydon, CR0 4YY

The paper used is Munken Premium, which is FSC certified.

Excerpt from *Lao Tzu, Tao Te Ching: A New English Version*, by Ursula K. Le Guin. Copyright ©1997 by Ursula K. Le Guin. Reprinted by arrangement with The Permissions Company, Inc., on behalf of Shambhala Publications Inc., Boston, MA. www.shambhala.com.

Poems by John Crook reprinted by kind permission of his family

Poem by Rupesh Shah reprinted by kind permission of the author

A CIP catalogue record for this title is available from

the British Library.

ISBN 978-1-908363-10-7

Foreword

The sea is terrifying. However bad things get they can always be 'worse at sea'. Storms and crashing tides transform that liminal seaside edge we associate with pleasure into existential crisis. We landlubbers, who stand ashore and wonder about the sea and its wild mysteries, also wonder about the motivation of those who venture out in small crafts. The world of charts, chandlery and tides, of wrecks, weather lore and navigation, so embedded in the languages of these islands, has a poetry which can seem arcane and remote. The sea itself – its bounty abused, its purity polluted – is now a source of environmental anxiety and threat. And yet, the romance of the open sea, its roving freedoms, its wilderness, sloshes through our imaginations like the shared tribal memory of mariners.

Of all the voyaging the sea calls us to, those undertaken by lone sailors have a unique resonance: the Dark Age peregrini casting themselves into waves in tiny coracles to find God; shipwrecked mutineers drifting in the hope of finding an island paradise; round-the-world yachtswomen and men pitting themselves against overwhelming odds to find fame; explorers, adventurers, fugitives – these are enduring tales because they travel beyond the far reaches of our own experience. Peter Reason has written his voyage not just as a sailor's yarn but as a thoughtful, challenging, moving account of a pilgrimage into wilderness.

Confronted by Nature at its most elemental, the intensity of the experience, the quality of the reflection and the humanity of the writing turn a journey from the south coast of England to the western isles of Ireland into an exploration of what it is to be human in the wilderness. At a time of increasing anxiety and environmental crisis, Peter questions how we live with Nature. Do we turn our backs on its troubling enormity or do we answer Nature's challenge: 'a wild call and a clear call that may not be denied,' as John Masefield put it?

This is a timely book of new British nature writing finding its sea legs within ideas of pilgrimage, ecological journeying, liminality of place, and essential engagement of self with the wild. This voyage is an adventure; it is also a conversation with Nature we can join as crew and feel the spindrift in our faces and the wind in our sails.

Paul Evans, Wenlock, (a long way from the sea), January 2014

For my grandchildren Otto, Liberty, Nathaniel, Aidan

That their generation may find a way of living
in harmony with Earth and her creatures

Which my generation has so conspicuously failed to do

Contents

IRELAND

Kinsale

ATLANTIC
OCEAN

CELTIC SEA CROSSING

PLYMOUTH TO KINSALE

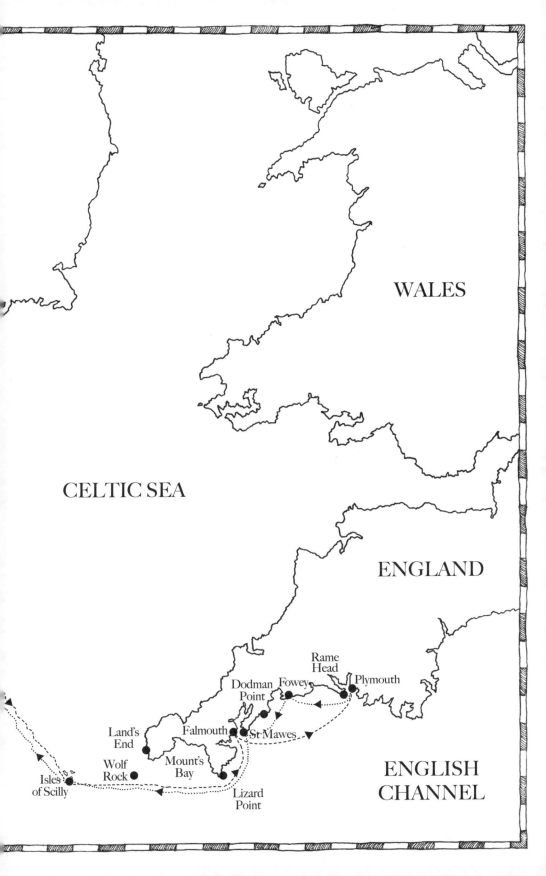

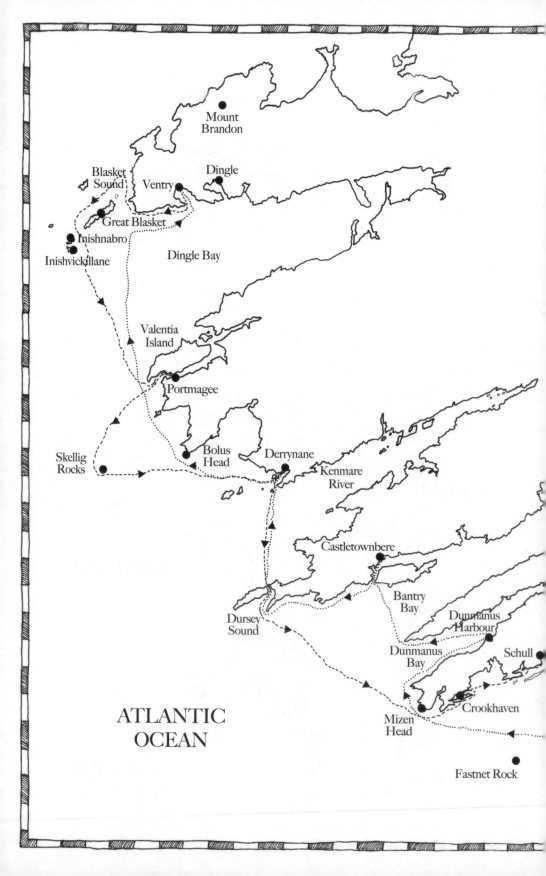

Mount
Brandon

Blasket
Sound
Ventry
Dingle

Great Blasket

Inishnabro

Inishvickillane

Dingle Bay

Valentia
Island

Portmagee

Skellig
Rocks

Bolus
Head

Derrynane

Kenmare
River

Castletownbere

Bantry
Bay

Dunmanus
Harbour

Dursey
Sound

Dunmanus
Bay

Schull

Crookhaven

Mizen
Head

ATLANTIC
OCEAN

Fastnet Rock

COASTAL PASSAGES

KINSALE TO BLASKET ISLANDS

Kinsale

Old Head
of Kinsale

Baltimore

Cape
Clear

CELTIC SEA

Chapter One
A Day in the Life

...if we do not hear the voices of the trees, the birds, the animals, the fish, the mountains and the rivers, then we are in trouble... That, I think, is what has happened to the human community in our times. We are talking to ourselves. We are not talking to the river, we are not listening to the river. We have broken the great conversation. By breaking the conversation we have shattered the universe. All these things that are happening now are consequences of this 'autism'.
Thomas Berry, *Befriending the Earth*[1]

I woke early and for a few minutes lay in my bunk savouring the warmth of the duvet. As Coral swung to her anchor, the low April sun shone through her windows, dancing oval patches of light around the cabin. I watched them lazily, then shook myself properly awake and climbed out of my bunk, stretching my stiff back and legs. In the galley, I pumped water into the kettle, lit the gas ring and set water to boil for tea, before clambering up the companionway into the cockpit to look around. Derrynane Harbour is a pretty bay on the north side of the Kenmare River, just off the famous Ring of Kerry on the west coast of Ireland, where the land rises steeply from the sea to the mountains. I had arrived in harbour two days previously after sailing around the Blasket Islands and Skellig Rocks, watching gannets nesting and meeting a pod of dolphins along the way. The bay is enclosed by low-lying islands, rocky reefs and sandbars, well sheltered from all directions. That morning, little waves were breaking on a beach behind me, lines of white rolling up over yellow sand. Ahead of me, coastal hills rose gradually toward the steeper mountainside, a patchwork of stone walled fields scattered with white houses and trees – more trees than one often sees on the west coast of Ireland. Above the fields, a clear line marked where the cultivated land stopped, and the scrubby brown of the mountains began.

It was still cold, the air clear and sharp – too cold to be outside in pyjamas and bare feet. Soon I was shivering, but stayed out long enough to notice there was only a trace of movement in the water, scarcely breaking the reflection of moored boats and the surrounding rocks and hills. Hardly a drop of wind. I was disappointed, even a bit grumpy, that there was no sign of the northeasterlies forecast the previous evening – I really wanted a good sail that day. Maybe the wind would arrive as the day woke up properly, as my wife Elizabeth likes to say.

I made tea – black Darjeeling, for the last of my milk had gone sour two days earlier. There was no fresh bread left and without milk I couldn't make the creamy porridge I had been enjoying each morning, but I found a packet of pitta bread in the dry food locker, toasted two pieces and spread them with butter and marmalade. It was several days since I had been near a shop. I tidied the cabin and washed my breakfast cup and the crockery and pans from last night's supper in a bucket of sea water. Before I'd set off, my younger son Matthew recalled our first family sailing trip to Ireland, nearly 25 years ago, saying with mock outrage, "You made us wash up in cold sea water!" Partly to conserve fresh water, but mainly to honour these memories, I was using sea water to wash up on this trip.

Those were the days when sailing holidays were part of family life, a way of having shared adventures and being a father to my sons Ben and Matthew, now grown men with children of their own. Mostly these were boys' trips, but Elizabeth joined us sometimes, especially enjoying three cruises in Ireland. Last time we were here she made a delicate pencil drawing of the Derrynane hillside I could see over Coral's bows.

But this time I was on my own, for I had a different purpose on this trip. During my career as a university professor I ran courses for management students on the challenges of sustainability[2] and led research into the adoption of low carbon technologies.[3] Now retired from university life, I wanted to look at the ecological challenge from a different, maybe more radical, perspective. I know from my professional life that there are all kinds of good ideas about how to make the way we live, our patterns of making and consuming, more sustainable. But I believe there is a deeper question: not only about what we do, but how we experience ourselves. We humans are, after all, just another species, an ordinary (and extraordinary) member of the community of life on Earth. It's just that we don't think of ourselves like that very often; we tend to see ourselves as separate, set apart from the organic whole that is life on Earth. Thomas Berry, a priest and theologian who wrote and taught about the deep connections between spiritual and scientific understandings of life, suggested that we humans have broken the great conversation between ourselves and the rest of the living world. What would it take to experience ourselves as participants in a wider, more-than-human world, in conversation with the sea, the land and its creatures?

Over breakfast and my morning chores, I looked back over my voyage so far. I had left Plymouth three weeks previously. My friend Gwen came with me as far as Kinsale, and then I sailed on west alone, visiting harbours and islands in County Cork and County Kerry, circumnavigating Great Blasket and Skellig Michael. It had been a kind of deep ecology pilgrimage, immersing myself in the experience of sea and coast, seeking a sense of participation with the more-than-human world. Now I was on my way home.

When I went on deck again, the wind had picked up, ruffling the surface of the water. I noted down the times of high and low tides, started the engine, hauled up the anchor hand over hand, grateful that I still found this less tedious than using the mechanical windlass, set Coral to motor gently into the wind while I hoisted the mainsail, and headed out of the harbour. I quietly thanked Derrynane Harbour for sheltering me in such beauty for two days, an internal ritual to honour the Earth. Now I was on my way again.

My plan for the day was to sail south across the wide mouth of the Kenmare River and through Dursey Sound at the end of the Beara Peninsula. I would then have the choice of tracking back east to Castletownbere at the entrance of Bantry Bay; or, if the wind were kind and stayed in the northeast, making one tack straight across to Mizen Head, the most southwesterly point of Ireland. I thought I might spend the night in Crookhaven just around the corner on the south coast.

I steered to line up the two beacons set on the shore at the entrance to Derrynane. They mark the leading line, the safe passage through the rocks that crowd around the entrance, and clear of the underwater hazards in the approach. It was a routine bit of pilotage, but I was attentive, focussed for a few minutes on the alignment and Coral's passage along it. Once away from the land I discovered a gentle breeze in the cold sunshine. Soon I was able to unfurl the genoa, or foresail, to balance the mainsail and set Coral on a gentle reach between Two Headed and Moylaun Islands out into the wide mouth of the river.

As I passed Moylaun, more of a low rock than a proper island, I was close enough to make out the horizontal division of the intertidal zone into separate little ecosystems. At the tideline, dark water and wet black rocks shaded into the rich brown of damp seaweed, swirling around in the gentle swell; above this, a tawny line of clinging barnacles; then naked rock, patterned with cracks, fissures and ledges in tones of grey, marked with splodges of white bird excrement; this shaded into a less regular line of bright yellow lichen; and the whole was topped by patches of emerald green spring grass. It was a pattern I had grown familiar with, common to all the rocks and islands along this coast.

Behind Moylaun I could see Deenish and Scarriff, proper chunky islands rising high out of the sea. On Deenish, the sun shone on a white house, tiny in the distance, standing alone above a narrow stretch of beach. The sharp light picked out the details of the gable end, the front elevation with its foursquare windows and the square dot of the chimneystack above. Far behind, away on the horizon, I just caught a hint of the Skellig Rocks. In my quiet aloneness on this trip I had grown to appreciate all the exquisite detail of the sea and coast.

It felt early in the day and early in the year. The air was cold in my throat and lungs. Although it was a bright morning, the sun was still low in the sky, throwing long shadows that gave texture to the land- and seascape. The world hadn't become flattened out as it can be in high summer. Looking east, into the sun, the nearer islands were dark silhouettes, with just a trace of detail in the shadow. Beyond, on the far side of the river above the line of reflected light dancing on the water, the mountains of Beara showed grey misty blue, darker but close in tone to the sky. I settled into a deep, if rather chilly, contentment as Coral lapped her way quietly across the Kenmare River.

• • • • • • •

Coral is a Rustler 31, designed by the celebrated Holman and Pye naval architects in the 1960s as a cruiser racer. She is very much of her time: low in the water, narrow of beam, fast for her size, even though solid and heavily built. In cross-section she is a traditional wineglass shape, with a long, deep keel ballasted with two and a half tons of lead, so different from modern yacht designs which tend to be more lightly built, wider and higher and so with much more internal space. At 31 feet, she is quite small and has cramped accommodation: just one main cabin for living and sleeping; a fore cabin with two extra bunks, which is usually crammed with spare sails and stores; and a deep, safe cockpit where most of the work of sailing takes place. Over many years of sailing I have become deeply familiar with her and fond of her idiosyncrasies.

We bought Coral as a family boat in the mid 1990s. After much searching for something that suited our needs and was within our budget I saw an advertisement for a Rustler 31 lying at Gosport. I was immediately attracted because the Rustler is the big sister of the Twister, a boat we had greatly enjoyed chartering in Ireland on two occasions. My elder son Ben and I went to Gosport and met the owner, Roger Wall, a man in his late sixties who had sailed her for many years. He rowed us out to Coral on her mooring, we climbed aboard and saw at once she was right for us. We knew from our research that Rustlers were solid and sea kindly, but were thrilled to discover she was such an elegant boat. The shape of her hull, the no-nonsense rig, the arrangement of the cockpit, all pleased us. When we went below we were delighted with the arrangements. What décor there was belonged entirely to the period in which she was built: quite plain but simple and attractive. The cabin was deep and the windows small, but with lots of white surfaces and pine woodwork it felt light and airy. A marine survey showed she was sound and within a few weeks we had agreed to purchase her.

We took Coral down to Plymouth later that spring and have kept her there on the same mooring for the past sixteen years. Over time I have made many repairs and improvements, including a new mainsail and boom, new instruments, an Aries wind vane and a complete refurbishment of the hull and deck. She is elderly but smart and businesslike.

Coral is a sloop, which means she has one mast, a mainsail and a genoa – foresail – which overlaps the mainsail. The mast is supported by steel standing rigging – shrouds and stays. The sails are controlled by rope running rigging – halliards to hoist them, sheets to control them. In the stern the cockpit side benches lift to access deep lockers where all the necessities of sailing are kept: pumps, mooring lines, boathook, spare anchors; engine controls; a large diesel tank; and all kinds of bits and pieces that might come in handy. The tiller, which steers the boat, comes into the cockpit through an opening in the transom – the flat stern of the boat – where it is bolted to the rudder, which hangs from the aft end of the keel. On each side are large winches that control the genoa sheets. The cockpit is sheltered by a red spray hood, now rather faded, and matching canvas dodgers showing 'CORAL' written in capital letters fixed to guard rails along each side.

Most of the sailing can be done from the cockpit, but I have to climb out and go forward to hoist the mainsail and reef it – reduce it in size – in strong winds. Right forward in the bows is the anchor, tied securely to the deck when not in use, with its chain leading over the anchor winch or windlass and down into the chain-locker.

· · · · · · ·

I had a peaceful and leisurely sail across the Kenmare River. The gentle breeze coming off the land scarcely ruffled the water. It slapped little waves against Coral's bow, which gurgled away under the hull and trailed behind in the wake. The day was unfolding well. With the wind seeming firmly in the northeast I promised myself another pleasant close reach across to Mizen Head. But first I had to negotiate Dursey Sound. I needed the genoa out of the way in narrow waters, so I hauled in the furling line that rolls it around the forestay and started the engine.

Dursey Sound is a narrow passage running north and south between the mainland and Dursey Island. Taking the Sound avoids the longer and often rough passage around Dursey Head, but because the tidal streams rush through fiercely it must be approached with care. I had worked out from the tide charts, carefully checking my calculations, that the south-going stream started at eleven, around five hours before high water. I had arrived as I planned just at the turn of the tide, maybe rather early after my quick sail across Kenmare River. The north entrance looked dramatic as I approached: a break in the line of cliffs, a stretch of turbulent water, sharp waves and streaks of foam where currents met. Along the tideline, the swell surged up the rocks sending out sheets of spray, then slowly ran down in rivulets of foam.

I knew the Sound would be quite straightforward to navigate in the quiet weather that day. However, the dramatic scenery brought with it a sense of caution and challenge. Anyone watching would have thought I looked cool and relaxed, but inside I was on high alert, checking rocks, course, speed, depth, the eddies of wind bouncing off the cliffs. Yet at the same time I was loving being here on my own in the drama of cliffs and waves. An underwater reef obstructs the middle of the narrows, so the sailing directions stress hugging the western side: 'There is deep water close to the shore so a yacht should keep very close in.' I steered as directed, wondering how close is 'close', keeping an eye on the depth sounder, which was finding no bottom at thirty feet. It was indeed deep. It felt weird to be sailing near enough the rocks to easily distinguish the individual feathers of the gulls and guillemots perched there.

With the engine driving her forward and the tide urging her from behind, Coral was soon past all the hazards. Ahead, beyond the narrows, the Sound opened up, the shoreline softened and the turbulence of the tidal stream died away. I breathed more easily as I passed the walled graveyard next to a ruined chapel on Dursey Island, exchanged waves of greeting with fishermen checking their lobster pots, stopped the engine and rolled out the genoa again. Coral sailed briskly, with a slight heel and a stronger gurgle under the bows, past Crow Head and out into the open sea. The expanse of Bantry Bay opened to the east, the vast Atlantic to the west. Southeast, I could just make out Three Castle Head then Mizen Head, twenty miles of clear open sea away.

But the wind had veered round, coming now directly from Mizen Head. Coral couldn't make the course I wanted; the best she could sail was due south. Then the wind began to fade away. After a frustrating time trying to sail and getting nowhere, reluctantly I started to motor. It was one thing to motor through the confined waters of a harbour or the Sound, quite another in the open sea: the engine was noisy; without the balance of wind in the sails Coral pitched uncomfortably in the waves; I was using fossil fuels; it felt all wrong. The recent high-pressure weather had brought sunny days, but frustrating, variable winds for sailors.

With no other boats in sight I went below to make my lunch. When I came back on deck a light breeze had picked up and, determined to sail if I could, I rigged the big No.1 genoa. I usually use the smaller furling genoa that is easily set by rolling it out from the forestay. The No.1 is more than twice the size; it fills the whole triangle between mast and forestay and sweeps the deck nearly back to the cockpit. It is a powerful sail, useful in light winds, but is more complex to rig – I had to go to the foredeck, rig the removable inner forestay and hank the sail on. Once it was hoisted and properly set, the big sail did the trick and Coral was soon making good speed, close-hauled on a course somewhat south of east.

When the boat is sailing close-hauled the sheets are winched in hard so the sails are set close to the fore and aft line of the hull and form an aerofoil shape, an elegant curve. The wind, as it flows across them, is forced to travel further round the convex lee of the sail than across the concave windward side. This difference of speed creates a low-pressure area behind the sail, so the boat is effectively sucked forward. To make the most effective windward course, the boat must be steered to point as close into the wind as is possible while the sails hold their aerofoil shape. Too close to the wind and the sails start lifting up at the luff – the leading edge – and eventually flapping about. Too far the other way and the sails simply block the wind: there is turbulence on the lee side rather than a clean flow, and the wind blows the boat over rather than sucking it forward.

I had all this aerodynamic theory in the back of my mind as I played around with the sheets that control the main and genoa, watching the shape of the sails, until I was happy Coral was getting the best from the wind. Then I made fine adjustments to Aries, Coral's self-steering gear. Aries is a traditional design of wind vane steering, hand-made to order from a small firm in Denmark, which can be set to steer the boat at a constant angle to the wind. A solid cast aluminium frame is strongly bolted to the transom, supporting a wind vane above and a paddle deep in the water below, connected by a clever set of gears and levers. The wind vane is adjusted by cords to sit upright, leading edge into the wind. Strong lines from the paddle run to the tiller to steer the boat.

When the boat goes away from the required course, the wind blows the vane over, and through the gearing this rotates the paddle in the water. The forward movement of the boat then catches the paddle and pushes it to one side, pulling the lines attached to the tiller and steering the boat back on course. The vane then comes back to the vertical allowing the paddle to return to its neutral position ready for the next adjustment. In actual practice the vane is in continual movement, so that Aries makes constant small adjustments to the course.

Aries is a simple cybernetic system, a cycle of information – wind vane, heading of boat, wind direction – which controls a cycle of power – the paddle pushed by the force of the water as the boat moves forward pulling the tiller.[4] Technically, this is a cybernetic system, a term derived from the Greek *kubernetes* – 'steersman'. It is never still because the 'correct' course to sail can never be predetermined: to be 'right', the system has to move in a direction which soon becomes 'wrong'; every action calls forth a reaction and thus corrective feedback. Aries works on the same principles as all natural ecological systems to maintain a dynamic balance around a zone of relative stability. Of course the great ecological systems that ensure the stability of populations, forests, oceans and the climate of the planet are far more complex, with cycles upon cycles of feedback. But I always delight in the elegance of this piece of ecological education that is attached to the stern of my boat.

Aries stands in as an additional crew member. Without it, all this single-handed sailing would be impossible. In most winds I can set it to steer Coral for hour upon hour, making continual adjustments, never tiring, never getting distracted, always following the wind. Unless of course something breaks – a line comes undone maybe, which it does very occasionally.

Particularly going to windward, when the relative speed and direction of wind and boat makes the cycle of information most sensitive, Aries will steer better, more consistently and in stronger winds than most human beings, and certainly for longer.

With the No.1 pulling well and Aries steering I was able to settle down in the cockpit for an hour while we sailed toward the coast. Maybe I became complacent. As we approached Three Castle Head I tacked Coral round and headed toward Mizen. Quite suddenly the wind freshened. For a few moments I was happy, as Coral picked up speed and charged on, but soon she was heeled over further than was comfortable, solid water over the toe rail and rushing down the side decks. Another squall whipped the tops off the waves into white horses all over the sea. I watched anxiously for a few minutes, then got to my feet in alarm as a surge of water nearly flooded into the cockpit. Aries was overpowered and Coral broached into the wind. My quiet sail had taken a dramatic turn. Rather too late I realized I had too much sail up.

Putting the big genoa up in light winds is one thing, getting it down in a squall is quite another. I started to hurry forward. But the foredeck was awash and sheets of spray were flying over the windward bow. "Careful, no need to rush!" I told myself, and used the time and routine of putting on full waterproofs, seaboots, lifejacket and safety line to calm myself.

What followed was half an hour or so of energetic gymnastics. While Aries kept the boat on a steady course, I eased the sheet to let the wind out of the No.1, went forward, hauled the flapping sailcloth down hand over hand and tied it to the rail. That was not too difficult. Back in the cockpit I winched in the roller genoa sheet to unfurl it. But the sail sagged on its stay and wouldn't set properly – I had to let the sheet out again, clamber back to the mast and tighten the halliard. Back to the cockpit again, I could now winch the genoa sheet so the sail set nicely. With the big genoa down the sails were properly balanced again and Coral was dancing safely through the waves. She is really happy in a good blow with plain sails set.

Once I had all that sorted and Coral was sailing well and safely again, I realized that when I came to tack again around Mizen I would need the No.1 stowed right out of the way of the furling genoa. Coral's movement was lively in the brisk wind, and each time I went forward I had to step up from the security of the cockpit between the sprayhood and the guardrails and half crawl along the side deck. To sort out the No.1 properly meant going right up to the bows, which were rising and falling three, maybe five feet with each wave. Sometimes the prow dipped into a crest so my hands were under water as I unshackled the sail and its stay. I crawled or shuffled around on my bottom on the soaking wet and steeply pitched foredeck. Each action – undoing a shackle, unclipping the stay, moving back along the deck – had to be done with, rather than against, the movement of the boat. I struggled to bring the wet and flapping bundle of the No.1 back amidships. As I lashed it to the guardrail some folds broke free and trailed in the water. I hung over the rail, suspended from my safety line, staring down at the water rushing past, dragged the heavy wet sail back on board and tied it down firmly.

With everything finally sorted I made my way back to the cockpit, warm and sweaty, rather out of breath, and settled down in the corner to rest. "I must look quite a sight," I told myself, sitting there in my ancient waterproofs, cheeks windburned, overlong hair soaked with salt water, and three weeks of grey, almost white, beard. I was pleased to be able to do all that at my age – sixty-seven next birthday – and that Elizabeth had not been there to watch.

All I needed to do now was continue south to clear Mizen and then tack east for the final few miles to Crookhaven. It didn't work out like that. I was impatient and tacked too soon, getting closer to the headland than was wise. The wind was now a brisk southeasterly and, blowing against the tide around the headland, kicked up short, sharp waves that knocked the way off the boat. On the old tack we had been going beautifully; on the new tack we made little headway. Maybe if I had sailed south for another half hour before going about I would have cleared the rough water and found a fast close reach to Crookhaven. But I was tired after a long and busy day, disheartened by Coral's jerky movement in these waves. The sun was going down and it felt too late to try that now. I furled the genoa, started the engine, and bashed through the waves toward Crookhaven.

· · · · · · · ·

In his essay *Good, Wild, Sacred*, the poet and wilderness writer Gary Snyder described the wilderness pilgrim's 'step-by-step breath-by-breath' progress into the wild, whether the wild of mountains or ocean or meditation practice. He wrote of this kind of pilgrimage as an ancient set of gestures that bring a sense of joy, a joy that arises through 'intimate contact with the real world' and so also with oneself.[5]

In some ways this had been an ordinary day in the life of a lone yachtsman: setting and changing sails, pilotage, watching the scenery, snatching lunch and a cup of tea, making good and bad decisions, reluctant motoring, finding a safe anchorage. Yet it had also been a day of making intimate contact with the world and challenging my sense of self. 'We are only talking to ourselves,' wrote Thomas Berry. 'We have broken the great conversation' with the world of which we are a part. Throughout the day, and through this whole voyage, I was seeking to re-establish a conversation with the sea and the land – a conversation that must start with good listening.

The first lesson from that day was about my 'self': how could I establish a conversation with the world if I was wrapped up in my preoccupations? Grumpy before breakfast because there was no wind; delighted with my morning sail in the cold sunshine; excited by the challenges of Dursey Sound; disconsolate that the wind didn't suit my plans; irritated that I had to use the engine. I was probably most present to myself and to the world when I was up on the foredeck single-mindedly struggling with ropes and sails on a wet, pitching deck. I found it a constant challenge to quieten my internal dialogue and truly attend to what was present.

When I did listen, one thing the wild world told me was rather obvious: it wasn't going to behave itself according to my needs or desires for a delightful day's sailing. It was doing its own thing. This was a lesson I didn't particularly want to hear. I was determined to complete the long hop around Mizen in a day, even with a bit of forcing from the engine. The wild world was pointing out that we are part of the whole and have to fit ourselves into it, not try to fit the whole to us. Snyder suggests that in this wild independence is our own freedom. We are only free when we take on the world as it is – sometimes painful, always impermanent – rather than how we would wish it to be. For in a fixed universe there would be no freedom.[6]

There is a parallel here with our wider culture. Somewhere in the development of civilization, Western people started to see themselves as separate from the natural world. This may even go back to the time of Genesis, for the notion that humans were placed on Earth by a Divine Creator, with a command to be fruitful, multiply and dominate the Earth, is deep in the collective unconscious of those brought up in the Abrahamic religious traditions. But there were many other influences – the invention of agriculture, the rise of cities and of dominant classes, the Renaissance view of man as the measure of all things. In particular the dualism of Enlightenment thought, as philosopher Mary Midgley so neatly put it, 'has been constantly engaged in separating individuals from their surroundings.'[7] A radical discontinuity developed between the human and other modes of being.[8] Those brought up in Western cultures came to see the Earth as a collection of objects available for human exploitation, rather than a community of which all beings are a part. In consequence we thought we could bend the world to our purposes.[9]

For many, but certainly not all, human life has become longer, less arduous and maybe more pleasant. However, as a direct result of this, we are devastating the planet. Contemporary arguments often focus on climate change. But we are seeing (if we are willing to look) a loss of biodiversity; the destruction of whole communities of beings; the destabilization of great ecosystems such as the rainforests and oceans; and the impoverishment of human communities.[10] The ruthless selfishness of the human species has driven the evolution of our extraordinary capacities; it is paradoxical that it may also lead to our own extinction and to that of most of the species with which we co-exist.[11]

Potentially this is ecocide,[12] even the death of the life process itself. If we could face it, it would be terrifying. But the ordinary human emotions of fear, anger, grief, even terror, are simply inadequate: most are simply numbed by the enormity of the crisis. Can any human being or society comprehend the destruction of the ecosystems within which we have evolved and on which we depend? Rather than terror, I often feel an unfathomable dread, an emptiness, a dull thud deep in the heart. In any event, negative feelings don't help; indeed, they lead to a sense of guilt and helplessness. We must be willing to face these dark challenges, but not be overwhelmed by them.

There are many things each of us can do to address the ecological crisis: buy less and buy more responsibly, drive less and more slowly, insulate our houses and turn the thermostat down, drastically reduce the number of flights we make. There are more things that industry and commerce can do, such as develop zero-carbon and cradle-to-cradle design and manufacturing.[13] There are many things our religious leaders could do to help us appreciate the sacred beauty of creation – and indeed many are doing so. And there are things that politicians could do: change tax and finance systems to stop rewarding ecologically destructive practices and reward benign ones; invest in low-carbon infrastructures and energy production; and so on.

However if, as I believe, the underlying cause of the ecological devastation is this sense that we are separate from the rest of creation, preventing and recovering from ecological disaster is fundamentally about human identity. Unless we change our view of who we are and our place on the planet, we are unlikely to find the energy and commitment to make the radical changes needed. In place of the discontinuity between the human and the more-than-human, we need to develop a profound and taken-for-granted experience of ourselves as participants, part of rather than apart from the community of beings that together make up the Earth's ecosystem. For we humans always live in relation with each other and the more-than-human world, glorious, flawed and temporary centres of awareness and action within an interconnected whole.[14]

In this voyage I set out to explore how might we again experience ourselves as participants in a wider, more-than-human world. How might we begin again the great conversation with the rest of the living world, and re-establish an intimate rapport with the Earth community? For the most important thing we can do is fall in love with the Earth again.[15]

• • • • • • •

Crookhaven is a deep narrow bay seven miles east of Mizen. After an hour or more of pounding into the waves I felt a familiar, happy relief as I steered Coral around Alderman Rocks into smoother water. I found a quiet place to anchor out of the wind in the shelter of Rock Island. Once the ship was settled and safe I poured a large (but carefully not too large) scotch while I boiled the last of my potatoes and warmed up a ready meal. I was in my bunk and asleep by nine, as I had been most nights of this voyage.

Chapter Two
Getting on Board

How does one organize an expedition: what equipment is taken, what sources read; what are the little dangers and the large ones? The information is not available. The design is simple, as simple as the design of a well-written book. Your expedition will be enclosed in the physical framework of start, direction, ports of call, and return. These you can forecast with some accuracy; and in the better-known parts of the world it is possible to a degree to know what the weather will be in a given season, how high and low the tides, and the hours of their occurrence. One can know within reason what kind of boat to take, how much food will be necessary for a given crew for a given time, what medicines will be needed – all this subject to accident, of course.

John Steinbeck, *The Log from the Sea of Cortez*[16]

Four weeks before my passage through Dursey Sound and around Mizen Head, I had taken the train down to Plymouth and a taxi to the boatyard where Coral was moored to the pontoon. I left her there for the shipwright to make some final repairs to the toe rail, which had been broken when she was lifted into the water. As I caught sight of her from the top of the gangway I paused with a moment of delight: I knew this little boat inside out, and there she was waiting for me to wake her up. Following the delight came a stir of anxiety, for this was to be a long trip, early in the year, and in parts totally on my own. What demands would it bring? Was I ready?

I clambered on board with my bags, drew back the hatches to let fresh air in, and settled into the familiar routine. First, I opened the seacocks and started the engine to check the batteries. Then I carried all the equipment that belonged on deck out from the cabin and put it in place: the blocks for the genoa sheets shackled in place to port and starboard; the winch handles placed ready in the cubby holes each side of the cockpit; the outboard engine clamped to the railing at the stern of the boat; and the danbuoy and

29

life ring installed ready to be swiftly thrown to anyone falling overboard. Then I hauled the No.1 genoa out from the forecabin and hanked it to its removable forestay, clipped out of the way to the side deck when not in use. With some difficulty I dragged the dinghy out of the cockpit locker – it only just fits – and lashed it down on the cabin roof.

Just as I pulled the last knot tight, I saw another taxi pull into the yard, and walked up the sloping ramp from the pontoon to welcome Gwen, who was coming with me as far as Kinsale. She got out of the taxi with a big grin and wide eyes, gave me a hug and immediately said, "I am so pleased to be here. I'm really excited about this trip." I warmed again to her presence, her ready smile, and her willingness to go along with whatever turns up. I was happy to welcome her aboard.

• • • • • • •

It had taken me quite a while to decide what kind of companionship and practical help I wanted for this voyage. I knew I needed a crew for the long passage across the Celtic Sea. However, single-handed sailing a yacht like Coral is perfectly possible so long as she is rigged up with good self-steering gear. The wind vane Aries is mainly for longer passages, so I also have an electric Autohelm for use in more restricted water. I keep it ready to hand so I can quickly clip it onto the tiller and keep Coral steady on a course while I hoist the sails at the mast, go right forward to prepare the anchor to let go, or simply to make a cup of coffee. Sailing single-handed, the important thing is to think ahead and take things slowly, so as not to be rushing back from the bows to get a winch handle or other piece of necessary kit left behind in the cockpit.

In many ways it is easier to sail on my own, certainly easier to do it myself than to explain what has to be done to people new to sailing. There are so many different names for ropes and other gear – sheets, halliards and kicking strap; winches and shackles; up-hauls and down-hauls; jam cleats, jack stays and lazy jacks. There are also many idiosyncratic arrangements on Coral that I designed and only I know how to use. Calling out instructions from the cockpit can be very frustrating for both parties. As the crew up at the mast tries to remember which rope to haul on, I find myself shouting from the cockpit, "Get hold of the main halliard, the one with the red flecks in it... no that's a reefing line. You need the halliard... goes up to the top of the mast... clipped to the toerail... No, no! not that red one, the other red one..."

Apart from these practical considerations, I find something deeply elemental about being at sea alone. I don't have to think social thoughts or attend to interpersonal relationships. I don't have to worry if others are happy, or feeling seasick. I don't have to explain myself. What happens is between me and the sea. I sit there, or move around the boat, watching the waves, gazing at the coast as it goes past, attending to the changing clouds and their relation to current weather patterns. I enjoy managing the boat, perfecting my own drills for tacking and gybing single-handed, sometimes pushing the tiller over with my bottom so I have my hands free to manage the sheets around the winches. I delight in my intimate relationship with Aries and the way I can balance sails against wind vane in the most effective setting. I love the quiet after coming into a bay and anchoring, or picking up a buoy in a harbour. On my own, the joys and the discomforts, the achievements and the mistakes, are all up to me.

I also delight in good company. My wife Elizabeth and I have sailed a lot together over the years. She is not a natural sailor. She often gets anxious, even frightened, and can be very seasick. When Coral starts to roll and pitch she tenses up as if she is trying to make the boat keep still. Elizabeth has no desire to join me on a long and challenging passage to Ireland, but chooses to come sailing in quiet weather, when she can delight in living on board, sailing along the coast, exploring coves and harbours. She tells friends that she wouldn't want to have missed the special experience, the privilege, of seeing the land from the sea.

Several years ago, cruising southwest Ireland, Elizabeth and I anchored in a rocky bay off Goat Island, County Cork. We were seeking out wild and desolate places. I had noticed this cove on the chart earlier, and wondered if it might provide some shelter from the cold north-westerlies that had been blowing all week. Reading the soundings, I thought the water might be too deep to anchor, but we agreed to go and have a look. We motored along the sound and out through the gap at the end of Long Island. Goat Island is a rocky outcrop rising some ten metres sharply from the sea with a thatch of rough grass on top. It is really two islands that only merge together at low tide, the two halves separated by a spectacular crack through the rocks only a few metres wide. Approaching from the sound, the island appears as one solid mass; then the crack gradually opens as the perspective changes, until the view is clear right through and back to the mainland.

We motored slowly into the tiny bay, carefully watching the depth sounder. For a moment the water shoaled to within anchor depth, but then plunged again to thirty feet and then more – beyond the range of the sounder. We crept up to the island, foot by foot, and close to the rocks suddenly found bottom again. "Let's try it here," I called, and Elizabeth dropped the anchor, letting all the chain out.

The anchor held, but felt precarious. It was presumably perched on a shelf of rock jutting out underwater before plunging to greater depths. We were very close to the rocks and Coral would not lie still. The wind whistling through the crack between the islands created eddies which swung her back and forth. Every now and then her stern would swing alarmingly close to the shore.

We turned off the engine, and for a moment experienced the silence of the world, a silence that lurked underneath all the sounds that remained to be heard: the wind in the rigging, the cries of birds, the pounding of the waves. It was a silence with a strange depth, infinite and yet so immediate we felt we could touch it. We looked up at Goat Island, at the rocky outcrops pushing through the turf. We saw a place not intended for humans, but for gulls and grass and a few wild flowers. We stayed there a short moment before our anxiety about the nearby rocks drove us away. Elizabeth hauled up the anchor and we inched gingerly back out to sea.

"That was rather special," I said as we motored away.

"Let's see if we have a moment of awe like that every day," Elizabeth replied, only slightly tongue in cheek.

We chatted about how you can't hold on to that kind of moment; it is there, you can acknowledge it, enter into it, but you can't take it away with you.

This is the kind of companionship I want on board Coral.

• • • • • • •

Gwen had sailed with me back from South Brittany last year. She has a very busy life as chief executive of a development organization that helps provide clean water to villages in Africa, but when I emailed her to ask if she might like to join me on this trip I got an instant reply, "Yes!" from her Blackberry. We soon had a phone conversation to confirm arrangements. I was really pleased when she responded enthusiastically to my invitation. She'd been good fun and happy in quite tough conditions on the way back from France. She knew her way around Coral, learned quickly, and was always willing to do what was asked. If confronted with a strange assortment of ingredients that was ready to hand, she could put together a far more imaginative meal than I ever could.

Gwen's original plan was to sail with me for two or three weeks, but a crisis in her organization demanded strong leadership to take it through very difficult times. While excited about the future she was clearly exhausted, and now could only spare ten days before having to fly back to Malawi. With more time available we could have chosen our weather opportunities, stopped for a couple of days to enjoy the Scillies and be well rested before the long hop across the Celtic Sea. But she could only come with me as far as Kinsale, and we had to get there in just over a week so she could catch her flight to Africa. After that, I would be on my own.

I took her from the taxi to where Coral was moored, we climbed on board and down into the cabin. Gwen stowed her clothes and other belongings into her lockers, I reminded her where things were kept, and we settled down for a long catch-up over tea and biscuits.

•••••••

From the cockpit, Coral's cabin is reached by stepping under the sprayhood and over the bridgehead – which keeps sea water from flooding below in bad weather – and down the companionway. Two steep steps lead to the top of the engine cover and another to the cabin sole – for some reason that is what we seamen call the floor. The companionway can be closed to keep the weather out by slotting in two washboards and sliding the hatch across, but mostly I keep it open. The cabin is deep and compact, half below the water level, and just tall enough for a six-foot man to move around without stooping too much.

On the starboard side is a narrow bunk behind which are lockers, some for food, some for clothes, and a bookcase crammed full – books about sailing and pilotage, novels and ecology books. Here I also keep the ship's poetry book, in which I ask everyone who sails with me to write a poem, either their own or one they know. To port is a second bunk, and stepped up behind it is a third, which we call the pilot berth. This is where bedding is stored during the daytime, but it also makes a safe and comfortable berth for a third crew member. All the bunks can be rigged with lee cloths or leeboards – raised sides to stop sleeping crew from falling out in rough weather.

At the foot of the companionway to port is the galley area, with a two-burner Calor-gas stove hanging on gimbals that keep it level however much the boat heels. Here there is storage for cutlery, crockery, saucepans and basic foods; a stainless steel sink and fresh water pump. To starboard is the aft-facing pilot seat and navigation table with space under the hinged lid to store charts. Above, the instrument panel has the log, which shows speed and distance travelled through the water, depth sounder, GPS (Global

Positioning System) receiver, which shows the ship's actual position by fixing on satellites, two-way radio and barometer. There are little drawers for spare shackles, nuts and bolts, bulbs, sailmaker's needle and thread and other bits and bobs that may come in handy. Under the pilot seat are bigger items, a bag of tools, oils, glues and miscellaneous 'bosun's stores'.

Everything has its place, although it is not easy for a new crew member to remember what goes where. Why does bread go in this locker while biscuits in that one? Why are tins kept in the aft locker under the port-side bunk but pasta in the middle one? Why are jams and sauces in the locker by the stove, and oils and salad dressing in the rack behind it? But everyone admires the cocktail cabinet, above the shoe cubby and below the household cleaning locker. The cabinet door opens downwards to provide a table to pour your drinks. Inside, the bottles sit safely in circular holes, with one specially shaped to take the square bottle of Gordon's gin. Behind the bottles the cabinet is lined with a mosaic of mirrored glass. It even has its own separate light inside. However much Coral heels and bounces around, you can be sure your booze will be safe.

I showed Gwen around and reminded her where everything was stowed. "It's all coming back to me from last year," she said. "It's amazing how you can fit so much into a space that is, what, about nine feet wide and twelve feet long?" She looked about the cabin. "How you have office, kitchen, dining room, saloon, bedroom, living area, storage, pantry all in the same place. And a glory hole where you can chuck stuff that doesn't fit anywhere else!"

This 'glory hole' is the forecabin, where two more bunks are slotted in under the foredeck with the anchor chain coming down the hawse pipe between them into its locker deep below the waterline. The bunks are not very comfortable and can only be used in quiet harbours because at sea the bows bounce around too much. On this trip the forecabin was entirely for storage – fresh fruit and vegetables in boxes, spare sails, large fenders and other things we needed to keep out of the way but have easy access to.

A narrow passage leads between the main and forecabins. To starboard is the hanging locker for waterproofs and to port the tiny compartment for the heads, as the sea toilet is called. This is very cramped, barely wide enough for a broad-shouldered man, and while there is standing room under the coachroof, the toilet bowl itself is partly tucked under the side deck. Raised above the cabin sole, bolted onto a platform so it fits in with the curve of the hull, it is slightly too high for comfort, for when sitting on it one's legs dangle awkwardly. I showed Gwen the two seacocks under the bowl that allow seawater in and excrement out, the pump that flushes water through, and reminded her how to switch the valve over to flush or empty the bowl.

· · · · · · ·

I always have a certain embarrassment about showing the heads to people new to Coral. Hard as I try, it is difficult to keep it smelling sweet, for the ventilation is poor. When Gwen and our friend Rupesh joined me to sail back from South Brittany, Coral had been shut up for a week. We jammed into the passage and peered inside. I sniffed the air cautiously to see how offensive the smell was. There was a vague whiff of stale urine mixed up with disinfectant – not too embarrassing – and some yellowish liquid sitting in the bottom of the bowl that I quickly pumped out.

I squatted down and scrabbled under the platform to show Gwen and Rupesh how to turn the sea cocks on and off. I showed them how to use the pump to flush the toilet bowl with sea water, where I keep the brush handy to clean the bowl out, and the toilet paper wedged into a cubby hole under the window. "Please make sure you put it back securely. There is nothing worse than finding the loo roll sopping wet on the floor, or fallen into the toilet bowl, just when you need it."

Rupesh noticed the piece of elastic cord around the toilet seat. "What's that for?" he asked.

"It's to hold the seat so it doesn't fall down while you're having a pee," I explained. "It's not always easy when the boat is heeled over, and you need both hands to aim straight. One thing worse than a soggy loo roll is having the seat fall down on you in mid-flow.

"When you come down for a pee and the boat is moving around a lot, remember to wear a hat," I continued.

Rupesh looked at me with disbelief in his eyes.

"You see, the only way to make sure you pee straight is to wedge yourself in. Set your feet against the bulkheads here, and jam your head in the top corner under the deck. But if you don't have a hat on these nobbly bolts that hold the window hurt your head."

I was sure Rupesh thought I was teasing him, but the first time he used the heads while we were sailing he came back up rubbing his head. "I see what you mean," he said, "it's not easy."

A few days later, after a long afternoon tacking to windward in a fresh breeze we were relieved to drop anchor safely in harbour. While Gwen and I prepared supper Rupesh sat quietly on the deck, scribbling in his notebook.

After a while he came down, wrote a fair copy in the poetry book, and read to us:

> Tight spot.
> Tilting starboard.
> Use head jam and lean to.
> Sharp angle threatens golden spill.
> Heads out.

• • • • • • •

Once she had settled in, Gwen wanted to know more about where we were going. I pulled out the charts of the south coast of Cornwall and Devon and pointed out the main headlands we would pass on the way to the Scillies: Rame Head, Dodman Point, the Lizard and Land's End.

"I suggest we go to Fowey tomorrow, that's an easy sail, about four hours. Then on past Dodman to the Falmouth area. The next hop is a long one, around the Lizard and on to the Scillies, that's twelve to fourteen hours with a fair wind and tide."

"I'm really looking forward to seeing the Scillies," said Gwen, "I've never been there."

"We can only stay a couple of nights if we are to get to Kinsale in time for you to catch your plane, but we should be able to see two or three of the islands." I found the large-scale chart of the Scilly Isles, which shows the main islands and the many off-lying rocks.

"We should be able to visit St Mary's, St Agnes and Tresco. Then there's the long passage across the Celtic Sea."

I pulled out the passage chart showing the sea area between Cornwall and the south coast of Ireland. "It's between twenty six and thirty hours, about the same as the crossing last year from Camaret to Plymouth."

Once we had finished looking at the charts, I put them back in the chart table in the order we would need them.

• • • • • • •

After my phone call with Gwen I was so pleased she could join me for this trip that I straightaway fetched the stepladder and climbed to the high cupboard where I store my charts. There was a pile of them nearly two inches deep. I pulled out six: the passage chart of the Celtic Sea between Land's End in Cornwall and the coast of Ireland and large-scale coastal charts of County Cork around to the Kenmare River in County Kerry.

Then I dug out my old copy of the *Pilot Book of the South and West Coasts of Ireland*.

A pilot book contains sailing directions for stretches of coast, indicating important features such as headlands and bays, and drawing attention to hazards such as hidden rocks and turbulence caused by tides. It will often suggest appropriate times of departure to ensure favourable tides on a passage. Pilot books are full of a remarkable combination of scientific information concerning tides and sea conditions and detailed instructions for entering ports and natural harbours. This is the accumulated experience of generations of local sailors and yachtsmen, all written in nautical jargon.

The *South Ireland Pilot Book* was first published by the Irish Cruising Club in 1930. My copy was the 1993 edition – nearly twenty years old and well used from four long cruises. Its spine was broken, the pages corrugated from being soaked and then dried. They were spattered with stains – coffee in some places, possibly spaghetti sauce in others. I read through it, reminding myself of earlier cruises. I discovered we had added quite a few marginal comments: at Adrigole in Bantry Bay we reminded ourselves to 'land at pier as top of bay smelly mud'; at Bantry Town 'very hard to see white post as not painted'; at Kenmare Quay 'Came up at ½ tide... withies off pier leave to starboard.' I wondered how much had changed and if I would need to invest in a new edition.

I turned to the charts and spread them out on my desk. I am a traditionalist here. I prefer Admiralty charts, printed on high quality paper, to the cheaper yachting editions. I have avoided electronic charts, which interface with GPS and so show the yacht's position in real time on a screen. They feel too remote. I like the physical feel of working my protractor across the paper and marking my position in pencil.

I pinned Chart 1123, the passage chart of the Celtic Sea, to my wall. It is like a map in odd reversal: land is shown in chunks coloured yellow ochre with only key features indicated. But around the coasts and out at sea the chart teems with information. Contour lines and soundings show the depth and nature of sea-bottom. Little arrows show the direction of tidal streams. Curly lines indicate races off headlands and overfalls where the tide flows over a shallow patch on the seabed creating turbulence. Lighthouses and buoys are marked by symbols, with the characteristics of their lights written alongside in code: 'FlG3s' next to a buoy at the entrance to Baltimore tells me it is a starboard hand buoy that will flash green every three seconds.

My old charts took me as far as the Kenmare River. How much further did I want to go? I certainly wanted to reach the Blasket Islands off the Dingle Peninsula. But as I looked at the distances and read the pilot book I realized that Galway and the Aran Islands were too far for the time I had available.

A few days later I found an opportunity to visit Price and Co., the nautical chart store, still in its old premises among disused railway lines and cranes on the Bristol harbourside. Going there is rather like travelling back in time – it's an old-fashioned shop with pilot books arranged on wooden book cases, and behind the counter a rack in which Admiralty charts in stock are laid out flat. It is also a shop with good old-fashioned service: I had a lengthy conversation with the gentleman serving me about which charts to buy. He knew his stock and made helpful suggestions as we looked at the catalogue together, and then brought out the alternative choices for me to examine. I spent a happy half hour looking through them, at the end of which I chose three charts that gave me both passage information and details of islands and harbours. I also looked through the latest edition of the pilot book.[17] While the sea and coast had changed little, I saw the book contained information about new marina and mooring facilities, helpful phone numbers as well as new, clearer chartlets and coloured photographs of harbours, so I bought a copy of that too.

Charts must be continually updated with changes to buoys and lights, depths, wrecks and other important information. The Hydrographic Office promulgates 'Notices to Mariners' – a wonderful phrase, both nautical and bureaucratic – which detail amendments chart by chart. New charts are updated to the day of purchase – there was a young woman by the window in Price and Co. painstakingly undertaking this task. I had to check that my old charts were still valid and update them. The Notices used to be published in a quarterly booklet, but are now available free on the Admiralty website. For chart 2129, for example, I found information about new fish farms, two rocks near the surface that no one seemed to have noticed before, and the deletion of a fog signal. I got out my fine pen and carefully marked these onto the chart in magenta waterproof ink.

Once I had made the corrections, these charts, while worn and based on old surveys, were in good order. But I was amused by a small cautionary note that I was instructed to affix to all my charts, headed 'Chart Accuracy':

Mariners are warned that positions obtained from Global Navigation Satellite Systems, such as GPS, may be more accurate than the charted detail, due to the age and quality of some of the source information.

Mariners are therefore advised to exercise particular caution when navigating close to the shore or in the vicinity of dangers.

'The map is not the territory,' wrote the Polish American philosopher Alfred Korzybski. By this he meant that we humans can only experience the world through our representations of it, which are always abstractions. The danger is that we then very often mistake these representations for the actuality.

In traditional navigation and pilotage one makes a careful estimate of the ship's position. Near the coast it is often possible to triangulate compass bearings of landmarks and get an accurate 'fix'. On a passage offshore, position is estimated by dead-reckoning based on distance sailed along a compass course from a known point, making allowances for tides and leeway. On ocean passages position is determined from astronomical observations. It is very easy then to assume that this estimate is factually true, forgetting that there are bound to be errors built into each measurement that may reinforce each other. One may even have botched the whole calculation. This problem can be amplified by modern electronic navigation aids, which through their very accuracy appear hyperreal, potentially giving the navigator a false sense of certainty. It is this that the Admiralty note was drawing attention to.

Korzybski's point is that we confuse map with territory on a much more profound level than this. Our entire view of the world and our place within it is based on largely tacit and unspoken assumptions about who we are and what kind of universe we live in.[18] We make a mental image of our world and then take it for reality, which then becomes the basis for our sensemaking and our actions. This is where the map/territory distinction becomes really important. For as the ecological educator David Orr argues, the disordering of ecological systems and of the great biogeochemical cycles of the Earth has its roots in an underlying disorder in Western ways of thinking, perceiving and imagination.[19]

This disorder arises from our tacit mental image of a world made up of discrete objects that can be manipulated separately. We are then surprised when we find out everything is actually profoundly interconnected. The fuel we burn in our motor cars and central heating boilers contributes to changes in the composition of the atmosphere and thus in complex ways to climate change; we spray our crops with systemic insecticide and then wonder where all the bees have gone. One of the great contributions of the modern ecological vision is to change our mental maps to show how life on Earth, and indeed the non-living world of rocks and atmosphere, all fit together in an intricate, ever-changing pattern.

I sat looking at my charts, enjoying the way this brief notice from the Admiralty had stimulated these reflections. As I voyage I shall explore the notion that the world is more alive, more sentient, more interconnected and more enchanted than is normally accepted in western civilization.

· · · · · · ·

As I tidied my charts away under the navigation table and Gwen and I were talking over our plans, we heard the sound of rain on the deck. It increased to a loud drumming, and started to blow down the companionway, so I had to close the hatch cover to keep the wet out of the cabin. We had thought of walking to the supermarket to buy last minute fresh provisions, but there was no point in getting soaked. It would be better to leave shopping until we got to Fowey. We spent the rest of the afternoon quietly reading and settling in.

As the evening drew in I poured us both a whisky. "What shall we have for supper?" asked Gwen, and she rummaged through the tins in the locker under my bunk. "These are a bit old, they need eating up," she said, checking the dates on a tin of vegetable curry and one of dhal. She put them together with another tin of ratatouille, added some spices from the ship's stores and served it all up on a pile of rice. Happily full, we started a habit that extended for the whole cruise of being in our bunks by nine and soon falling fast asleep.

Chapter Three
Setting Out

Huckleberries and salmon call for bears, and clouds of plankton in the North Pacific call for salmon, and salmon call for seals and thus orcas... So the question I have been asking myself is: what says 'humans'? What sucks our lineage into form? It is surely the 'mountains and rivers without end' – the whole of this earth on which we find ourselves more or less competently at home. Berries, acorns, grass-seeds, apples, and yams call for dextrous creatures something like us to come forward. Larger than a wolf, smaller than an elk, human beings are not such huge figures in the landscape...
Gary Snyder, *The Practice of the Wild*[20]

We woke to a morning of rain and low cloud. I climbed into the wet cockpit and looked down the river. The water was still, the lines of yachts on each side of the river reflecting dully in the early morning light, while the red and green navigation buoys that mark the deep passage stood out sharply.

After a quick breakfast Gwen and I dressed up in seaboots and full waterproofs. Mine are old and wearing rather thin, but I resist buying new ones partly because of the cost and partly because I rather like the shabby look. I feel I might look like a novice in spanking new ones. Gwen wore the smart newer set I keep on board for women crew. It was raining quite hard when we got into the cockpit, and she laughed as she turned the high collar up and pulled the hood over her head so all I could see was her nose and eyes peeking out. Dressed up like that she could take a full wave over her and still be dry underneath.

We let go of the mooring lines and motored down the river past the familiar sights: the cargo ship unloading road stone at the commercial quay; the camouflaged landing craft at the Marine base; the crowded yacht masts in the marinas, the Citadel towering over the waterfront. Gwen went forward to the mast to hoist the mainsail, hauling up the slack of the halliard hand over hand and then tightening the luff with the winch. There was practically no wind, so we kept motoring across Plymouth Sound. The clouds were clinging so low that we could not see into Cawsand Bay on the western side nor to the headland beyond. For a few moments we wondered if the visibility was too poor for us to continue, but as the rain shower passed the headland became clear and the pastel colours of the waterfront houses of Kingsand and Cawsand glowed warmly under the low cloud.

I scribbled some notes about the weather: 'grey clouds fall down onto a grey sea...' "There are not enough different words for grey," I complained to Gwen, starting a conversation about colour that continued over the next few days. We agreed the sea was a gunmetal, greeny grey, flecked with the occasional white wavecap; further west it turned steely blue with a metallic sheen on the surface. When we looked carefully at the sky we saw that its grey had hints of brown and even purple. The only saturated colours were the navigation buoys; everything else was washed out by the mist in the air. "There are no pure pigments," said Gwen, "even the buoys lose their brightness in the distance."

I was happy to be started at last. I relaxed into the familiarity of Coral's movement under my feet, feeling my weight move from one foot to the other to meet the slight roll of the hull. This was calming, for I was no longer anticipating the voyage: we were on our way. The previous weeks had been busy getting Coral ready: painting her bottom with anti-fouling; seeing her launched from the boatyard where she spent the winter; rigging the sails; bringing on board the cushions and bedding stored at home through the winter against the damp; filling the tanks and spare cans with fuel and water, buying and stowing stores. The food lockers under the bunks were crammed: tins of soup, beans, tomatoes; packets of various pastas; jars of sauce; spare tea and coffee. Fresh food – butter, cheese and milk – was stored in the coolest place next to the water tank under the cabin sole, along with two crates of beer and some bottles of wine. Fruit and vegetables were in baskets in the forecabin, bread and biscuits in their lockers, sauces and spices next to the galley area at the bottom of the companionway. A selection of easy to cook food and snacks for long passages – instant soups, pasta and pesto, chocolate, bananas, dates and apples – were kept ready to hand. There was more food on board than we could possibly need, but it gave me a feeling of security. We could stay at sea for weeks if need be.

I had enjoyed these preparations, while underneath I remained anxious. This was an ambitious voyage to be undertaking so early in the season, for after Gwen left me in Kinsale I would be sailing single-handed on the west coast of Ireland, fully exposed to the Atlantic Ocean. Even though I had been looking forward to this trip for several months, I was concerned about leaving home for so long. Planning a voyage is so very different from actually doing it. My nights had been restless, troubled by dreams of charts and passages, sometimes of emergencies at sea.

In the most dramatic of these, my imagination would run riot. I would vividly experience a crisis, working step-by-step through the emergency routine, sending out a Mayday message:

MAYDAY MAYDAY MAYDAY

This is the yacht Coral Coral Coral

Mayday Coral

Five miles south of the Lizard Point

We have hit a large floating object and are sinking

Two adults on board

We require immediate assistance

Over.

When I woke up I realized I was in my bed and Coral was safely on her mooring. But I could go on like this for hours, dropping off to sleep and dreaming up yet another crisis that never happened. I experienced these imaginary dramas in vivid detail: I felt the wind in my hair, the ropes in my hand, saw the precise arrangement of tiller and winch in Coral's cockpit, the curve of the mainsail reaching above me. Yet these crises were always far more frightening than anything that I had actually experienced. Now we were at sea the uncertainties faded; perhaps they hinted at an unspoken fear I was not attending to.

I remembered Gary Snyder's comment, that human beings are 'not such huge figures in the landscape.' We are not such huge figures in the seascape either. We are about the size of a dolphin, far smaller than a whale, tiny in comparison with the wind and waves of wild weather. Were we sufficiently dextrous for this big trip? What called us forth on the sea? How did we know when conditions would be right? Experience and expertise can be reassuring, but every time we set out we are confronting the untamed, unpredictable sea in a very small boat.

• • • • • • •

Gwen and I motored past the Plymouth breakwater into the open sea and turned west toward Fowey. Out of the Sound we picked up a modest wind from the south. Although the water surface was smooth, a slight swell rolled across the sea. For a while Coral picked up a long-legged gait, rolling gently with each wave, the bubbling noise of the bow wave rising and falling as she lifted and dropped. Passing Rame Head a sliver of blue sky appeared amongst the mottled grey, still a little washed-out through thin clouds. We played with the notion that it was shy and might disappear altogether if we stared at it too long. As we sailed across Whitsand Bay toward Looe the sliver slipped around the sky, appearing here and then there. Gwen laughed, "It's almost flirting with the clouds."

Off Looe Island the wind died away and I started the engine, motoring closer to the coast past Talland Bay and Polperro. Above us the clouds broke up and the sun shone warmly through, while darker clouds clung over the land, fluffy below but merging into layered stratus above. In places the cliffs were smothered in gorse; in others a dusting of blackthorn reached down to the water. Sometimes the two mingled so that the slopes were woven tapestries of golden yellow and off-white, contrasting the fresh spring green. Passing Polperro I noticed how the white houses stepped down the hills on each side of the harbour, set about with dark green, almost black, Scots pines. The cleft in the rocks leading to the narrow harbour entrance came into view for just a few moments as we passed. I tried to catch a glimpse inside, remembering, as I do every time I pass this way, the family holidays we had there. My Mum and Dad always took us on a seaside holiday when we were children, making great efforts to find a place that was in some way special, even in those years of post-war austerity. It was on these holidays that my fascination with boats, water and the sea began.

• • • • • • •

It all started when I was six. We rented the motor yacht Sinbadia on the river Avon at Christchurch as a holiday home. I was excited to sleep on a boat, and my imagination was caught as I read the brass plaque in her cabin that told me she was one of the 'little ships' that had gone to Dunkirk to rescue British soldiers. I spent countless hours sitting in Sinbadia's tender, always moored to the landing stage because I was too young to be allowed to go rowing on my own. Dad showed me how to tie her up with a proper knot: a round turn and two half hitches. I remember dreamily pulling her back and forth through the water, watching the ripples form from her tiny bow-wave.

A few years later – I must have been nine – we went to Polperro, taking the Watch House as a holiday home. We were quite a big party. There was my Mum and Dad, big sister Ann and brother John, me, our cousin Suzie; and our family friends Wendy, Bill and their daughter Lesley, a year younger than me and my best friend at that time.

The Watch House stood right by the water, the walls rising directly out of the harbour bottom. At high tide the water lapped just below ground floor level, while at low tide it retreated, leaving behind sticky mud and gravel. Outside, a small terrace was separated from the harbour by a low stone wall with bright orange marigolds growing along the top. At the end of the terrace a small slipway, a slope of stone and concrete, led down to the harbour bottom. We would all sit on the terrace in the sunshine and watch the water creep in with the rise of the tide. One day, when the tide was high, John announced he was going to build a boat and paddle it around the harbour.

In those days, small boys who wanted wood to make something would go to the greengrocer and beg for some orange boxes. We would carefully take them to pieces, trying hard not to split the thin planks as we pulled them away from the more substantial ends, keeping the nails to hammer straight for re-use. We only ever got them sort of straight, which made woodwork much more challenging. I remember setting off together through the narrow streets of Polperro to find a friendly greengrocer, then leaving John to do the talking. We were in luck and came back with two nice boxes.

John said we should keep one of them pretty much intact, just removing the middle partition so there was space enough to climb in. We knocked the other box to pieces and used the planks to carefully cover the gaps to make our boat watertight. Somewhere we found some black, tar-like substance – probably oil washed ashore from a ship – and used this to caulk the joints between the planks. It wasn't so much a boat as a floating box.

I don't think this took us very long to do, but we hurried to finish as the tide was coming up. It was late afternoon when we launched our boat, around teatime, with the whole extended family party – quite an audience – gathered to watch on the terrace.

Put into the water, our boat floated magnificently. Not much water came in and it bobbed about beautifully. John put on his swimming trunks, paddled into slightly deeper water, and clambered in. The boat turned over immediately, tipping him in the water. He tried again and again. It tipped up every time. Amid much laughter, it was suggested that maybe I could do better as I was smaller and lighter. Full of confidence that I would show up my big brother, I clambered in. I too was immediately capsized into the cold water. However hard we tried and whatever we tried, the same thing happened.

45

We have a few pictures in the family album of all this, but more importantly the story of John's boat is imprinted in the minds of everyone who was there. Nearly sixty years later I mentioned I had recently visited Polperro to my cousin Suzie. "Do you remember John's boat?" she said immediately, "wasn't that a hoot?" Lesley still remembers she laughed so much she was nearly sick.

John went on to build some proper boats that really did float. One was a simple collapsible rowing boat, which we tested very early one morning among the rather startled ducks on the pond at Wandsworth Common in London where we lived. It held us both with no sign of tipping up, but we were chased off by the common keeper when he came on duty. Later John built a folding canoe, a great success on many expeditions. One holiday in Wales our parents let us paddle it right around a headland to a distant beach – I am appalled to think we did this with no knowledge of tides, and no lifejackets or other safety equipment.

These holidays by the water gave me my taste for the sea. As I grew up I read as much as I could about ships and sailing. I saved up over birthdays and Christmases to buy the set of C.S Forester's *Hornblower* stories of the Napoleonic wars. I got hold of a library copy of the enormous tome *The Log of the "Cutty Sark"*,[21] which accounted for every detail of her story, and was gripped by accounts of rounding Cape Horn with sea washing right over the decks. When I was about eleven I discovered Arthur Ransome, and lived in fantasy the adventures of the *Swallows and Amazons* in the Lake District, the Broads, and on the high seas.[22]

I also built lots of model sailing boats, with wooden hulls, which I painted carefully, and sewed sails from worn sheets on Mum's old, hand-cranked Singer sewing machine. When I was old enough I took them on the bus up to the Round Pond in Kensington Gardens. My boats never seemed to sail straight, so I would anxiously watch them as they tacked back and forth in the middle of the pond, taking forever to return to me.

I didn't get into sailing seriously until I was grown up and my two boys were old enough to learn to sail dinghies. Our first boat was a modest Mirror dinghy – you can still see their red gaff-rigged sails everywhere. One of our earliest adventures, on holiday with my father, was mackerel fishing off Hope Cove in Devon. We launched from the beach, set out along the coast and trailed the line with feathered hooks behind. To our surprise, Matthew soon felt a tug on the line – we had hooked two big fish. Towing a mackerel line with two struggling fish on it made the little boat quite unstable, and by the time we had them on board and knocked them over the head we had slippery scales and blood all over the bilges. It was all a bit more of a challenge than I had reckoned on – two small boys and a boat full of mackerel – but we caught six lovely fish altogether, which the boys took triumphantly home to Grandpa for supper.

We grew out of the Mirror and moved on to larger dinghies and then on again to chartering small yachts, learning as we went along but also taking appropriate training courses in sailing and navigation. In time we were confident and skilled enough to sail to France and Ireland.

Sailing with Ben and Matthew became an important part of my fathering and the process of growing up together. It was the time of the men's response to the women's movement. I had read many books about men and masculinity including Robert Bly's *Iron John*[23] and Sam Keen's *Fire in the Belly*[24]; been on a workshop with Robert Bly; formed a men's group with five friends. Bly argued that in contemporary society boys remained too close to their mothers and too distant from their fathers. Sailing together was one way to counter this. It was important that we had boys' adventures together, often taking one of my grown-up men friends along for company. But it was also important that we shared the ship's housekeeping, learned to look after each other when things got tough, and above all to trust each other. I well remember lying in my bunk half asleep and wanting to remain so, listening to Ben and Matthew consider the best course to avoid a big ship or some other hazard and deciding they knew what they were up to. Trusting my mid-teen sons with our safety was an important part of growing up – for all of us.

•••••••

Polperro slipped behind us and we carried on along the coast. Gwen went below and fell asleep, exhausted after the challenges of the past weeks. Past Udder Rock buoy and the sands of Lantic Bay, the entrance to Fowey harbour opened up: the red paint of the leading light bright against the rocks on the western cliffs; the grey stone of the fort below, built in the time of Henry VIII to guard the entrance; the low rocks marked with a cross on the eastern side of the river. Along the western side of the river, white Victorian and Edwardian houses line the hillside over the older muddle of buildings that is the site of the medieval trading town. I chose a visitor's buoy, steered into the stream, clicked the engine into neutral and walked forward with a boathook to pick it up. I was pleased to catch hold of it first time, not always easy to judge on one's own. I slipped a mooring line through the ring on the buoy and secured it to the cleat on the foredeck. After stowing the sails and making all secure, I woke up Gwen with a cup of tea.

Chapter Four
Along the Coast

Evolution proceeds as an unscrupulous, opportunistic comedy [...] Successful
participants in it are those who live and reproduce even when times are hard
and dangerous, not those who are best able to destroy enemies or competitors.
Its ground rules for participants, including people, are those that also govern
literary comedy: Organisms must adapt themselves to their circumstances in every
possible way, must studiously avoid all-or-nothing choices, must seek alternatives
to death, must accept and revel in maximum diversity, must accommodate
themselves to the accidental limitations of birth and environment, and must prefer
cooperation to competition, yet compete successfully when necessary. Comic
action, in literature or in natural history, follows naturally from these principles.
Joseph Meeker, *The Comedy of Survival*[25]

Fowey is a natural deepwater harbour. To this day large ships visit to load with china clay from the Cornish mines at a wharf just above the town. A wide section of the river is kept clear for these ships, but to each side the river is crowded with moorings for local yachts and visitors. In high season the visitors' moorings are packed, with yachts rafted up two or three to each buoy. But it was early April, most moorings were vacant and Coral swung to her buoy on her own.

Once we were settled, and had gone ashore in the dinghy for our shopping trip, Gwen and I napped on our bunks for a while, tired from the busyness of setting out, and from the unaccustomed amounts of fresh sea air we had been breathing. That evening, over fish and chips in a town pub, we chatted about sailing experiences and the conversation turned, as it so often does, to rough weather.

• • • • • • •

I was fast asleep in the pilot berth when Kate, my son Ben's girlfriend, woke me.

"Ben says can you come on deck and help him take in a reef," she said, very calmly and with no sense of urgency.

We were sailing home across the Bay of Biscay after a cruise of northwest Spain. The weather seemed settled. This was our first season with Coral and we were pleased she was seaworthy and in good order. We had set off in high spirits, soon settling down to the routine of watchkeeping, chatting and sleeping, on what we expected would be a five-day voyage back to Plymouth.

Matthew was asleep in the bunk below me; Ben was on watch with Kate. It was her first long-distance passage. I had left them happily sitting in the cockpit enjoying the night sail. The wind must have got up a bit.

I dragged myself out of sleep, grumbling to myself about why he couldn't reef on his own, and began systematically to put on waterproofs. But I must have been too slow.

"Hurry up, Dad!" came a more urgent call from the cockpit, and as I looked out a flash of lightning lit up the cabin. Instantly wide-awake I was up the companionway, looking around. Blinded by the lightning, everything was pitch black. Then another flash, and I could see the sea surface all around us covered in windblown foam and spindrift. The wind was from dead aft, and the mainsail was pressing on the shrouds as if about to burst. It was dark again for a moment, then another flash erupted.

Ben was struggling with the tiller to hold Coral on a safe course. At any moment she might broach across the wind and waves. No time to take in a reef, I was up at the mast, letting the halliard free from its cleat, hauling down handfuls of mainsail, bundling it anyhow around the boom. As I worked I realized that Matthew was alongside me, woken by the noise and rushing up to help.

With the mainsail secured we clambered back to the cockpit and furled the genoa, rolling it right down around the forestay. Even with no sails set Coral was still pounding through the water, and with each flash of lightning we could see the white foam of her wake merging with the windblown surface of the sea.

We had been overtaken by a thunderstorm, with its sudden and violent squalls. I guessed the storm was on the leading edge of a low-pressure system that had formed and deepened quickly off southern Spain and was now moving fast north and east. The next shipping forecast was scheduled several hours away. We had to guess how the weather would develop.

Kate was clearly alarmed by the sudden change and out of her depth. I told her to go below and get safely into a bunk. Matthew went below as well, and Ben and I took watch together over the next couple of hours, keeping Coral on course before the wind and assessing the conditions.

The thunderstorm moved past us and with it the violence of the squall. The wind dropped, and we were able to hoist the mainsail again, this time well reefed down. I checked our course against the chart, and found that we could sail safely with the wind on our quarter, keeping well away from the French coast. We had plenty of searoom and for the moment were quite safe.

Over the next few hours the wind force increased again, and with it the height of the waves. Waves are formed by the action of the wind on the water surface. The stronger the wind, the longer it blows and the greater the 'fetch' – the distance the wind has travelled over the surface of the water – the bigger the waves. We had no wind speed indicator in those days, so had to make an estimate from the state of the sea, which is notoriously difficult. With first light we could see the waves and began a conversation that went on intermittently for the next two days.

"How strong do you think the wind is, Dad?"

"Stronger than anything we've been in before."

"Do you think this is gale force?"

"I don't know, they say yachtsmen always overestimate the wind strength. I think it must be Force 7."

Force 7 is a near gale. I got out the almanac and checked the definition on the Beaufort Scale. Force 7 winds are 27-33 knots and the waves are around five metres high. I read out loud:

"Force 7. Sea heaps up. Some foam from breaking waves is blown into streaks along wind direction. Moderate amounts of airborne spray."

"It's at least that."

The waves kept building. Every now and then one would rise up over the stern of the boat so that from our seats in the cockpit we were looking up at water curving above us. Most of the time Coral would quite happily raise her stern and allow the wave to pass underneath. I realized that the ship was perfectly able to handle these conditions so long as nothing broke. We were going in the right direction. The most important thing was to make sure the crew were safe, warm, rested and fed.

We settled Kate into the pilot berth where she was tucked up safely and out of the way of running the ship. She stayed there for most of the next two days. Ben, Matthew and I agreed a rota: we would have one person taking short watches in the cockpit, a second person always ready to come on deck quickly, while the third had a proper rest. Anyone going on deck would have full waterproofs, boots, lifejacket, harness and safety line. Since there was spray flying around, and every now and then a bigger wave would break right over the cockpit, we slotted in the washboards and pulled the hatch cover so water couldn't flood down into the cabin. It was lonely work at the helm.

It was also hard physical work, as the big seas coming over the quarter would slew the stern around to starboard and then back to port as they rolled past. Each one of us, when it was our turn at the helm, had to tune into this rhythm, so that without thinking we could anticipate the movements and steer a reasonably straight course. After a couple of hours, arm muscles began to ache.

We needed to eat and drink to keep our energy up, but cooking was out of the question. We snacked on what we could find. I was on watch one evening while the others got some food together. Ben slid back the hatch and stuck his hand out, offering me a bowl of cold baked beans with three sardines balanced on top and a slice of bread. It was just what I needed.

Over the next day we ran before an increasing wind. We climbed onto the cabin roof to reef the mainsail down further and rolled in more of the genoa. Coral was still sailing too fast, surfing down the waves until it seemed that we would plough into the back of the one in front. Fearful that she might sail herself under a wave, we took the mainsail right down, lashed it securely to the boom, and continued with just a tiny triangle of the genoa. Still we rushed on.

Once we had ourselves and Coral properly arranged for the weather it was surprising how quickly we settled into a routine. Our initial alarm over, we began to look with greater openness and appreciation at the sea around us and listen to the sounds of the wind and the water.

That night two of us were sitting in the cockpit, gazing at the dim light of the compass, carefully holding our course. From time to time a wave broke over us. There was a moment of comparative silence which, we learned, meant a wave was curling above us and waiting to break. Then the thunder of solid water hitting the deck. Curiously warm, it crashed on our backs, streaming over our waterproof hoods and down our jackets. Gallons of water sloshed noisily around the side decks, pouring into the cockpit well, swirling around our boots. And then relative quiet again, just the sound of water trickling down the drainage channels and streaming through the cockpit drains back out to sea.

In the light of day, the sounds became less dominant. The wind had eased off somewhat, although the waves had built up considerably. As each one reared over the stern we could look up into its curving underside. For several moments it would be a sense of colour that predominated, for as the wave prepared to break it turned from dark grey to deep green and then to a translucent turquoise streaked with white. Poised above us it was arrestingly beautiful. Then it lost its form and its colour, breaking into a mass of foam.

We also started to watch the birds, tiny ones we had not seen before. They were fluttering on the downwind side of the waves, legs walking along the surface and beaks darting in and out of the water, gathering food. So long as they stayed in the lee of the wave they were out of the wind and in relatively calm water. But every now and then one of them would get too close to the top of the wave, the wind would catch them, and they would be blown downwind away from us, presumably to find another wave to feed behind. Checking our bird book we found they were storm petrels, no more than 25 centimetres long and very light. They feed on the sea creatures that are churned up by the waves.

One might assume that crossing Biscay in a gale in a small boat called for heroics. But what was really needed was calm, clear-eyed attention to the wind, the sea and the boat. There was nothing to be heroic about. And some incidents were comic, at least in retrospect.

At dawn after two days of gale or near gale, Ben and I realized that at last the wind was dropping back to a strong breeze. Coral had slowed down and we needed more sail. The sea was still rough and the cloud was low, closed around us, so visibility was poor. I clipped on my harness and lifeline and clambered up to the mast. As Ben turned Coral toward the wind so I could hoist the sail, I caught sight of a cargo ship right behind us. It was lucky that we had turned at that moment, for we had actually steered out of its path. The ship passed us, so close that even through the mist we could read the name on her bows without using binoculars.

Of course we should have seen it. But after a long and tiring night, I was furious. I stormed down the companionway, and called up on VHF radio Channel 16.

"Biscay Carrier, Biscay Carrier. This is Coral, Coral. Over."

"Coral, this is Biscay Carrier. Go ahead." The voice was calm and clear.

"Did you see us ahead of you? You are the overtaking boat! Our right of way! Are you keeping a proper lookout?" I spluttered.

"What are you so upset about? We missed you, didn't we?" came the laconic reply.

The balloon of my indignation completely deflated, I hung up.

Through that day the wind kept dropping. The gale passed us. We even hoisted the spinnaker for our last day crossing the Channel. Kate was able to get out of her bunk – she was tired and sore from being rocked around and pleased to be on her feet again – and put together a feast of curried vegetables. We sailed into Plymouth rather pleased with ourselves.

"Where have you come in from?" we were asked at the marina where we called in for showers and a hot breakfast.

"Oh, we've just come across Biscay from Spain," we replied modestly.

"Good crossing?"

"A little bouncy at times."

• • • • • • •

When literary theorist Joseph Meeker writes that survival depends – in life as in literature – upon taking a comic rather than a tragic perspective, he doesn't mean that adventures like this are necessarily funny, although at times they may be. Instead, comedy is about responding to events as they actually are rather than how we might wish them to be. Comic action seizes the moment and playfully adapts to circumstances while not taking yourself too seriously. Tragic figures in literature and history cling to their self-image and pursue single-pointed achievements, which can lead to heroic self-sacrifice. They attract admiration even in failure – as, for example, does Captain Robert Falcon Scott's death in the Antarctic. In contrast, comic figures such as Yossarian in Joseph Heller's novel *Catch 22*,[26] who rejects questions of right and wrong in the interests of survival, are viewed with amused suspicion. Yet such characters survive and adapt, while tragic figures bring about their own suffering because they commit to a course of action that must inevitably lead to their own doom.

Looked at like this, the comedic way is an evolutionary necessity, essential for survival in a complex and interconnected world, a world that you cannot control and know you cannot control. To survive, even to thrive, you have to be awake, pay attention to what is happening with wide-eyed awareness; you have to be present in the actuality of events, rather than thinking about what should be or how you would like things to be; you have to keep options open and not make unnecessary all-or-nothing choices.

Caught up in a gale in the Bay of Biscay, we had to make the best of it. I didn't mean the first cruise in our new boat to involve crossing Biscay in a gale. And I wouldn't do it again out of choice. But we learned from this experience that we could trust Coral to look after us in heavy weather. We saw that her limits were probably beyond ours. It was scary at times, but in the end, it was actually fun.

• • • • • • •

Overfull with fish and chips, Gwen and I made our way back through the narrow streets of Fowey to the pontoon where we had moored the dinghy and fired up the outboard to cross the river to Coral. Streetlights reflected pools of orange in inky black water. The noise of the outboard thrashed the air and the dinghy's wake disturbed the stillness. A line of cedar trees marched in silhouette along the ridge above the town, a deeper black than the sky behind. Coral lay quietly at her buoy. We reached her, stopped the engine and through the silence we heard owls hoot in the woodland up Pill Creek opposite the town.

The next day there was no wind. April is usually a transitional month in which the Atlantic depressions that move over the waters of Great Britain begin to track northwards as the days lengthen, giving the characteristic sunshine and showers – the kind of weather forecasters call 'changeable'. Depressions, low-pressure systems, arise at the boundary between warm wet tropical air and cold dry arctic air. A finger of warm air intrudes into the polar air and because of the temperature difference starts to rise. As it does so, Earth's rotation causes it to spin anti-clockwise and move east. It develops into a mature depression heralded by a warm front – with lowering cloud, increasing winds and rain – and a trailing cold front that brings polar air and clear skies. As a depression crosses the country it brings a familiar pattern of winds over the British Isles – they back southerly as it approaches; veer southwest to west between the warm and cold fronts; and finally west to northwest as the cold front passes. Of course, there may be a string of depressions passing or other complications to this characteristic pattern.

However, this spring there were no rain-bearing depressions, no succession of April showers; it was turning out to be among the driest and warmest on record. High-pressure had settled over the western Channel, bringing light winds and fine but hazy weather. Winds rotate clockwise around high-pressure systems, often bringing cold and dry northerly or easterly winds. The strong pressure gradient between low- and high-pressure systems can bring very strong winds. But in the middle of the high there are no such gradients and so no wind. Some climate scientists are suggesting that the melting of Arctic ice is both slowing down the jet stream and changing its path. It no longer flows in a steady eastward stream but in looping meanders that block the usual changeable pattern so that one kind of weather – like this high pressure – persists.[27]

"We'd better push on to Falmouth anyway," I said to Gwen, "the tides are flowing westerly during the daytime, right to take us around Dodman."

Dodman is the next major headland after Fowey. It is important to go with the tide around headlands, because the mass of water pouring out of the bays on each side means the tidal stream is stronger.

"How do you work out what the tides are doing?" she asked, and we sat down with the almanac and tidal charts and did the calculations together.

The pattern of tidal streams develops where the Channel meets the Atlantic. The moon and the sun pull on the oceans creating high and low tides around the planet. In mid-ocean the range of the tide is relatively small, but in the narrow seas between England, Ireland and France, huge quantities of water are funnelled into restricted space, surging in and out to create larger tides and strong streams. The basic pattern of streams is east and west, up and down the Channel, but is distorted by bays, headlands, islands and estuaries. The Cornish Peninsula, protruding into the Atlantic and dividing the Channel from the Irish Sea, creates particularly complex patterns.

I have a book of tidal flow charts that show this pattern through the whole cycle, from six hours before high water to six hours after – direction arrows marked on an outline of the coast. I showed Gwen how to look up the tide times in the almanac, correct for British Summer Time, and enter them on the page for high water. We then turned the pages and entered the time for HW+1, for HW-1, and so on forward and backward until we could read off the state of the streams at any time of the day.

We could also see how the flow in each direction begins gradually, picks up speed, then slows again; how an area of slack water, where there is no stream, moves up and down the channel as the tide turns; how the tide is strongest past the major headlands and weakest in the bays. I explained to Gwen about the races and overfalls where there can be rough water at the major headlands, caused by the mass of water rushing out of the bays.

"See at the Lizard, the arrows show that as the tide changes the water is still flowing southeast out of Mount's Bay as it starts to flow southwest from Falmouth. These two streams of water meet off the headland and can cause very rough water for a while." There are lots of wavy lines on the Admiralty chart off the Lizard to indicate the possibility of overfalls.

"And you can see from these thick arrows, which indicate strong streams, that the westward tide around Dodman starts about seven this morning and lasts till mid-afternoon. We should leave by eight at the latest."

· · · · · ·

After breakfast we motored out of the river and set the Autohelm on a course for Dodman Point – there is no point in steering by hand with the engine going, and it was more fun to look around. In the absolute calm the log – which shows the speed of the boat through the water – and the wind speed indicator read exactly the same, showing that the only wind was caused by the movement of the boat.

Gwen decided that today the sea was silver blue.

"What kind of silver?"

"All kinds of silver," she replied with a grin.

"It's rather like a dimpled mirror," I added.

We passed Gribben Head with its red and white striped daymark startlingly clear against a pale sky. Ahead, the dark length of Dodman was decorated with clouds of all shapes and shades of grey, cumulus gathering below sheets of stratus. The low sun in the east caught the daymark and the tops of clouds. Looking out to sea the horizon was scarcely distinguishable as sea faded into sky.

"Now the sea is like shining satin," Gwen told me, "and the sky is velvet. When you look toward the sun, the sea has all the colours of shot silk, while toward the land it is cold and dark."

As we approached the Point itself, two cormorants surfaced just ahead of Coral. They swam vigorously out of the way, bodies underwater, leaving a wake on the calm sea. Then one after the other they dived, flipping their bodies up to follow their heads under water. There was a slight disturbance on the water where they had disappeared, a pattern of concentric rings that soon merged with Coral's bow wave and were gone. Four gannets flew past in low formation.

I am particularly fond of Dodman Point. The towns of Mevagissey and Goran Haven shelter on its eastern side, then it stretches a long low finger into the Channel, always seeming to me dark and mysterious. I looked up at the small cross, sharp against skyline, which marks the top of the cliff before it slopes jaggedly down to the sea. In this flat sea, with the gathering tide behind us, it was safe to pass close and watch the rocks change shape as we went by. Beyond Dodman the coast is exposed, with rough cliffs and deep bays, but as we continued into the shelter of Falmouth Bay and the Lizard the land sloped gradually down to the softer and cultivated Roseland Peninsula. I gazed at the fields and hedges as we ambled past. There must have been centuries, maybe millennia, of human dwelling and cultivation here. The farming is still on a small scale, but huge compared with that of the original Neolithic farmers. I imagined the life of early inhabitants, farmers, fishers, gatherers. This must have been an attractive place to live in prehistoric times, with the richness of seafood and the relative warmth of a maritime climate.

This western entrance to the channel has long been significant in the history of seafaring, as the old sea song suggests:

> We will rant and we'll roar like true British sailors,
> We'll range and we'll roam o'er all the salt sea.
> Until we strike soundings in the channel of old England;
> From Ushant to Scilly 'tis thirty-five leagues.[28]

It was in these seas that Drake encountered the Spanish Armada; pirates from North Africa raided the coastal towns of Cornwall and Devon for slaves; the *Mayflower* set off with the Pilgrim Fathers; the British Navy went forth to rule the waves. Across these waters the ships and landing craft of the Allied forces invaded Normandy. Here, the first major oil spills happened: the *Torrey Canyon* ran onto the Seven Stones reef between the Scilly Isles and the mainland in 1967; the *Amoco Cadiz* ran onto the Portsall Rocks off Brittany in 1978; both did enormous damage. And through these waters a significant proportion of world trade still pours. Huge ships bring oil, gas, and consumer products from all over the world to the markets of Europe.

John Masefield wrote in his poem *Cargoes* of the 'Dirty British coaster with a salt-caked smoke stack,/Butting through the Channel in the mad March days...' Not so long ago there would have been jetties and small harbours in all rivers and inlets around the country for the coasting trade. These are now rotting away, or converted for pleasure and tourist use. In this not so distant past, many more people made their living by the sea, fishing, in coastal trade, smuggling. Now it is my privilege to sail for pleasure, and the sea trade is dominated not by dirty coasters but by huge ocean container ships. It seems to me that Masefield's poem needs updating:

> Over-sized container ship, all the way from China,
> By GPS to Felixstowe to fill the Christmas shops,
> With a cargo of smart phones,
> Football boots, machine tools,
> Shiny children's bicycles and cheap party frocks.

I went up to the foredeck, away from the noise of the engine, and looked over the sea, gently undulating in front of me away into Falmouth Bay. A speck of brilliant white on the surface ahead caught my eye. It disappeared, reappeared, settled in my vision. As it passed Coral I looked down to see a feather, floating concave side up, tiny, downy at the base, held up completely dry by the surface tension. It bobbed about in the bow wave and disappeared behind us.

The engine was pushing us through the water at five knots, but the GPS indicated that we were travelling over the ground at over six – we still had more than a knot of tide behind us even now we were past the Dodman in more sheltered waters out of the mainstream We were at the period of spring tides, which occur twice each month just after the full or new moon. At these times the gravitational pull of the sun and the moon is in alignment, drawing a larger surge of water around the planet so the tidal range is higher and the streams stronger. Neap tides occur in between at the half moon, with a small tidal range and weaker streams.

I was surprised at the strength of the stream today even for springs. Checking the almanac more carefully I saw that this spring tide had one of the largest ranges in the whole year. These big tides are called 'perigean spring tides', and are caused by the elliptical orbit of the moon. They occur three or four times a year when the moon is at the closest point to Earth (its 'perigree'), so its gravitational pull is greatest and is aligned with the sun. I remembered reading in the papers that the moon was making an unusually close approach to the Earth this month.

For a small yacht such streams are very strong. Coral can sail in favourable conditions at a maximum of about seven knots, although cruising we are likely to average around four or five.[29] Two knots of tide will reduce or increase the actual distance covered by nearly half. But more than this, the tides interact with the wind and the shape of the land. The water flows faster and is more disturbed off headlands and in shoal water; and, if it runs against a fresh wind, short, steep waves are thrown up which can make progress in a small boat uncomfortable or even impossible. Traditional sailors with less access to diesel power would have paid far more attention to tidal conditions, anchoring-up to wait for favourable tides.

On a long cruise like this one I find I grow into the rhythm of the tides. I know where I am between springs and neaps, have a sense of when high and low water will occur each day even though I may not have looked up the exact time. I become more patient with the constraints the tidal streams place on my sailing, willing to get up at the crack of dawn to catch an early tide, or wait through the morning for a favourable later one. The tides offer a great lesson in Meeker's comedic practice – living with, rather than against the rhythms of the world. It is quite different from hurtling down a motorway, sealed away in comfortable warmth from natural forces, so we scarcely notice if we are going up a hill. But I don't always find it easy to be patient. Sometimes I find myself pushing against a tide, or thrashing through overfalls past a headland. These occasions have always been uncomfortable rather than dangerous, but serve as warnings that natural forces will not be mocked.

We would need to be careful rounding the Lizard, since the big tides would cause more turbulence in the water even in this quiet weather. The sailing directions recommend passing three miles to seaward. But the same tides bring a great advantage on the long passage out to the Scillies. There is a particular quirk in the pattern of tides: the ebb flows west around the Lizard and Land's End for six to eight hours as water drains out of the Channel. We could pick our time of departure so as to have a favourable stream all the way.

• • • • • • •

St Anthony's Head is at the end of the Roseland Peninsula, forming the eastern side of the entrance to Carrick Roads, one of the largest natural harbours in the world. The lighthouse is obscured from the east, but as we rounded the head it came into view, perched on the rocks just above the high water line: a white octagonal tower surrounded by what were once keepers' cottages and, nearby, the storeroom for the oil that fuelled the light. Today the nineteenth-century tower supports a modern automated light which is an important navigational aid for the approach to Falmouth: a red sector shows over the Manacles, a dangerous reef halfway out to the Lizard and the site of many shipwrecks.

We chose to drop anchor in St Mawes on the eastern side of Carrick Roads, opposite Falmouth, for it was quieter and more sheltered from whatever easterly wind might blow up. It's a pretty town that stretches along the side of the inlet behind a sea wall. As usual with Cornish villages, the houses by the sea are smaller and older, originally cottages for locals, while above and around them are large Victorian and Edwardian mansions, built for visitors when the railways opened up this part of the country. St Mawes Castle, another of Henry VIII's constructions, protects the entrance. We had no trouble finding a spot to anchor clear of the moored yachts.

The chain rumbled over the windlass, slowing as the anchor found the bottom. I took Coral astern to lay more chain along the seabed. Happy that she was secure, I turned off the engine and we sat in the cockpit, enjoying again the quiet noises of the sea and the faint rumble of traffic and voices coming over the water from the town.

Chapter Five
Interlude at St Mawes:
Memories and Reflections

*Plumbing and philosophy are both activities that arise because elaborate cultures
like ours have, beneath their surface, a fairly complex system which is usually
unnoticed, but which sometimes goes wrong. In both cases, this can have serious
consequences. Each system supplies vital needs for those who live above it.
Each is hard to repair when it does go wrong, because neither of them was ever
consciously planned as a whole. There have been many ambitious attempts
to reshape both of them, but, for both, existing complications are usually too
widespread to allow a completely new start.*
Mary Midgley, *Philosophical Plumbing*[30]

After tidying up and having lunch, Gwen and I took the dinghy
ashore and spent the afternoon walking the coastal path around
the Roseland Peninsula to look at the lighthouse and the beaches.
Leaving the dinghy well above the high tide mark we scrambled up the
bank from the shore, and followed the path along the side of St Mawes
harbour. It took a varied route: along the bottom of a field beside a hedge of
bramble bushes; over a stile and under pine trees; high above a beach, then
low where a bridge crosses a marshy place, before climbing steeply to the
high cliffs overlooking Falmouth Bay.

On our way we passed a heron standing stock still in a rock pool,
surrounded by glistening brown seaweed. Its reflected image jumbled
curiously with the limpets and sea anemones clearly visible at the bottom
of the pool. The banks and hedges each side of the path were full of
wildflowers: bluebell, daisy, violet, apple, gorse, blackthorn, stitchwort,
toadflax.

After the steep climb we found a place to sit looking down over the bay.
The sea was pale turquoise, hazy white toward the horizon, merging with
the sky. It was flat calm, the ships anchored in the bay lying this way and

that, smoke rising vertically from their funnels. Gwen told me a bit more about her work in Africa and the funding she was hoping to secure on this next trip, about the challenges of being a chief executive and her passion to create an organization that fits its purpose. And she asked about the influences that brought me to ask the kind of questions I was bringing on this voyage.

•••••••

I have been asking questions about the state of the Earth all my life, and have often been dissatisfied with conventional answers. In part this comes from being brought up a Nonconformist. My family was closely associated with the Congregational Church; my paternal grandfather had been a minister and leading figure in the Christian Socialist movement; my father's elder sister wrote children's books about the London Missionary Society; and my mother and father met through the Church. Every Sunday we went to the brick Victorian Gothic building that was Balham Congregational Church. My father was a deacon. We sang in the choir. My mother did the flowers. Much of my family's social life revolved around the church, its bazaars, its clubs, its scout troop.

But we were never unquestioning believers. Congregationalism is based on the premise that the governance of the church should be in the hands of the congregation. I was brought up to a more radical view that it was up to each individual to make their own choice as to what to believe. My father would report fierce disagreements with the minister about religious dogma such as the virgin birth, the trinity, and the resurrection; and about the form of worship itself. The whole family would pick over these at Sunday lunch along with our dissection of the sermon that had been preached that day. As a small boy I loved these disputes.

Our attitude was probably close to that of the eighteenth century Deists. We were scornful of those who accepted religious doctrines laid down by authority and yet felt there was some purpose in this extraordinary world we inhabited. We didn't not believe in God, but doubted if He (this was before the days when the women's movement suggested we might think of God as 'She') had any relevance to the challenges of living a good and moral life. We took these challenges seriously, however, and considered it a human duty to work out the way to live a good life.

None of this was actually made explicit. To a large extent we were a middle class family living according to conventional norms. Throughout my childhood my parents were preoccupied with re-establishing normal family life after the deprivations and disturbances of the Second World War. My mother was probably more conventional in her thinking, more inclined to douse curious questions from us children. But nevertheless, it is this spirit of questioning that I value most from my childhood. It seems apt that the story my father most loved to read to us was from Kipling's *Just So Stories*, about 'The Elephant's Child' who cannot contain his 'satiable curtiosities'.[31] "What does the Crocodile have for dinner?" asked the Elephant's Child, and asking this question got him into trouble when he actually met the Crocodile on the banks of the great grey-green greasy Limpopo River. He had to be rescued by the Bi-coloured Python Rocksnake. While asking questions could be dangerous, it should also be protected.

As an adolescent I embraced Nonconformism as part of a necessary rebellion. My refusal to kneel in prayer or bow to the cross in chapel fuelled wonderful and furious arguments with the Headmaster and Chaplain of my relatively high Anglican school, although I happily sang in chapel choir and loved the music. I took great delight in finding scornful arguments to show the fundamentalists of the Bible Society the foolishness of their views. By the time I reached university this Nonconformism had hardened and my attitude of questioning faded. I proclaimed I was an atheist and could be unpleasantly opinionated.

I chose to study Economics. Somehow I thought this would help me learn to think, but of course it didn't. I remember sitting in an early lecture in which supply and demand curves were drawn on the blackboard. "We hold everything else as equal," said the lecturer, meaning to say that it was not relevant to the theory. "But everything else is not equal, the things that are not equal are the things that really matter," I thought to myself, and never took my undergraduate studies seriously again. After graduating I joined a large multinational company to pursue a safe and rather ordinary career in personnel management.

My spirit of questioning was rekindled when I became drawn into the company's organisational change programme. Management and unions were working together, redesigning jobs and pay structures to make them more appropriate for educated employees operating complex modern chemical plants. In business terms, this was aimed at greater effectiveness. But in addition, by replacing repetitive manual work and close directive supervision with jobs that required judgment and independence, it appealed to ideals of human dignity and responsibility. I was young, idealist and naïve, but I had for the first time in my life found an issue that chimed with the social concerns I had been brought up with.

It was the late 1960s. Elizabeth and I were just married. We lived a comfortable life in the pretty town of Dollar, nestled under the Ochil Hills in mid-Scotland. I had a steady job in a good company, we had a nice house and sports car. Elizabeth was training as a teacher. We seemed to be very settled.

But this was the Age of Aquarius, the time of 'Peace, Love, Freedom, Happiness', as the rock musical *Hair* put it. Even in middle class life in rural Scotland some aspects of the counterculture seeped our way. We learned about the US Civil Rights Movement and the opposition to the Vietnam War. We heard about Woodstock, about the countercultural guru Timothy Leary's instructions to 'tune in, turn on and drop out' and wondered what he meant. We went to see *Hair* in Glasgow and found the freedom it expressed – the naked bodies, the loud rock music, the irreverence, and yes, the wild hair – stimulating. Through my work we got to know several organization consultants from the USA, and they held a strange attraction to both of us. They commanded what seemed like huge consultancy fees while managing at the same time to carry a countercultural aura around them: cool, interpersonally open, challenging norms. They introduced us to 'sensitivity training groups' and 'encounter workshops', intensive experiences designed to encourage people to be open and direct in their relationships with each other. We both participated in such groups and were touched by the possibility of a more open and less rule-bound way of being in the world. 'Authenticity' was a buzz-word at the time; it challenged the 'buttoned-up' style of British life.

My American friends encouraged me to make a radical move. They told me about the Organizational Behavior doctoral programme at Case Western Reserve University in Cleveland, Ohio, at that time the leading graduate centre for organization development work. I wanted to follow them into the exciting world of organization consulting. I wanted to learn more about the theory and practice of social change. I wanted in some way to be part of this emerging counterculture that promised to turn the world upside-down. Elizabeth felt the same way; we both wanted an adventure in our lives. It was this strange, confused, idealistic bundle of ideas that, after much heart-searching, led us to sell up, leave our careers, and move to America.

• • • • • • •

Gwen and I continued our walk along the cliff, past the observation hut and gun emplacements left over from the Second World War. The path led between high banks, so soldiers could move around under cover. The banks were still covered in wildflowers – now we spotted red campion, primrose, lady-in-the-pulpit, oak, celandine, bladderwort and thrift. We followed a sign pointing us to a bird hide, a rough hut where we sat and looked through slits across a cleft in the cliffs. Below us the sea swirled around; above, the grass-covered clifftops; in between, a vertical exposed rockface. Somewhere here, according to a notice, a peregrine falcon was nesting. We stared out across the gap, searching the ledges, tiny openings, tufts of grass. We tried following the instructions in the exercise book that had been provided, where birdwatchers had noted their observations: 'to the left and down from the patch of white rock.' But which patch of white rock? Seeing nothing after half an hour, eyes tired from squinting, we made our way back along the footpath, carried the dinghy down to the water and returned to Coral.

Back on board we listened to the evening shipping forecast: still little wind, and the suggestion of 'fog later'. I had no intention of sailing to the Scillies if there were any chance of fog, so we might have to stay in St Mawes another day. It was a bit of a downer after our pleasant walk. The prospect of waiting around filled me with gloom. I had enjoyed our walk, but my back had started hurting, I felt tired and the overwhelming challenges of the trip kept returning to me. The sailing was fine, Coral was fine, we were doing well. Yet every time we stopped I wondered if I would find the energy for the next leg. I phoned Elizabeth. It was her birthday, and even though we had agreed it was OK for me to be away, she was clearly disappointed with me for not being with her. I missed her, and felt torn between the comforts and responsibilities of home and the challenges of sailing.

Gwen cooked a fantastic supper, making quite ordinary food – sausages, potatoes, lentils – into a bit of a feast using just one pan. She let the ingredients simmer together so the different tastes mingled, and added a judicious touch of paprika. After supper and washing up I went on deck while Gwen dealt with her emails.

It was a really quiet night. With no wind, and Coral lay still on her anchor, riding to the tide, water trickling past. The full moon peeked though broken cloud for a moment, and then the sky was overcast again. Across the river the lights along the waterfront were bright, but many of the houses up the hill remained dark – holiday lets, unoccupied so early in the season. The calls of children playing late came clearly across the water. I couldn't stay gloomy with all this dark beauty around me. Tomorrow would bring what it brought: 'sufficient unto the day is the evil thereof,' as my father used to say.

We set the alarm to catch the early shipping forecast: wind variable Force 3 or less and fog all along the southwest coast of England. The local radio station confirmed that the Scillies would be fogbound all day. We made a snap decision to stay put, and went back to sleep. As ever, the weather brought a lesson in comedic living in the world: go with the moods of the planet, not against them. We had no sensible option but to make the best of waiting.

Gwen slept soundly until past nine; she was really tired, and another quiet day would be good for her. After breakfast we decided to go back to the hide, this time with binoculars and the telephoto lens on my camera, and see if we might spot the peregrine.

• • • • • • •

America was a shock. The heat, the noise, the abruptness of social manners, the pervasive sense of violence all disoriented us. The Cuyahoga River, which runs through downtown Cleveland, was so polluted in those days it had caught fire the year before we arrived. The predominantly Black area of the city between downtown and the University was still scattered with burned-out houses – the scars of race riots some five years earlier. Our new American acquaintances delighted in frightening us naïve English newcomers with stories of muggings. It took us both quite a while to settle. It was easier for me, with a readymade community of graduate student colleagues and regular classes to go to, than it was for Elizabeth, particularly since she was unable to get a teaching job as she had expected. The turning point came when, at the end of the first semester, we put our fears to one side, bought an old Rambler station wagon for $75 from one of our new friends, and bravely took off for New York and Boston to spend Christmas with my brother and his wife.

In the midst of this confusion – we called it 'culture shock' in those days – I was uncovering new ideas and my own intellectual capacity in quite unexpected ways. I was blessed with an extraordinary teacher, Professor Nathan Grundstein, known to all as Grundy. He will always be for me a wonderful example of the American secular Jewish intellectual. Short, with greying hair, peering out through heavy spectacles, he seemed fascinated by everything, living with an appearance of continual inquiry – which he pronounced, in his nasal American accent, as 'INquiry' with emphasis on the first syllable. We first encountered him at a departmental party when he introduced himself to Elizabeth and asked her, in his intense way, what it was she did. Elizabeth, still unsure about where she was going to fit in with life in America, nevertheless had the presence of mind to reply, "I'm learning how to live in your country," a response which delighted him.

At our first class I sat with my fellow doctoral students around a square of tables in a graduate seminar room. We were still anxiously sniffing each other out: who was like us, who was not? Where might be the friendship and where the competition? Grundy came in and introduced the class by saying, "You guys and gals must all be pretty smart to be here. Tell me something about what you know."

One after another we ventured something we had learned from our professional experience, or of ideas we had picked up from fashionable ways of thinking. Each time, Grundy would gently but persistently ask, "And how do you know that? How can you be sure?" Within an hour he had laid horribly bare the un-thought-through assumptions we carried – what philosopher Mary Midgley would call the 'hidden plumbing' – in particular our uncritical adoption of humanistic and countercultural attitudes. We all found this challenging. Some of my co-students were outraged at this questioning of what they saw as their fundamental beliefs. I learned to love it.

Grundy would tell us, "Most people are very careful what they put in their mouths. I am very careful about what I put in my mind." He was particularly concerned to uncover underlying assumptions and structures of thought, what are often called 'worldviews' or 'paradigms.'[32] As Mary Midgley puts it, these worldviews are not literal descriptions of how the world is, but 'imaginative visions' which capture the basic assumptions about who we are, what kind of universe we live in, and what is ultimately important to us.[33]

What I learned with Grundy sowed the seeds of much of my future work. I realized that scientific methods, exploring the world through analysis, measurement and experiment, envisioned a world of separate objects, of inanimate things and the human mind as separate and privileged. But this was often inappropriate for exploring human experience, for human persons are self-evidently not objects but subjective beings whose actions arise at least in part from their understanding and intentions. The existential world of persons requires a different inquiry approach from the empirical world of things. It took me several years to see that this insight applied also to the more-than-human world.

One day, toward the end of my studies at Case Western, I was walking down Adelbert Street through the middle of the university campus, puzzling about how to approach my dissertation research into personal relationships. None of the available social science research methodologies satisfied me. They all placed me as researcher outside the relationship: I was trying to work out how to understand relationships from the inside. I can still, 35 years later, remember the thrill of the realization: instead of seeing myself as the researcher of other peoples' relationships, I had to turn the whole idea of research upside down and invite people to become researchers of their own lives. My job was not to answer questions for other people, but to create a space that would stimulate their curiosity and discovery.

I soon discovered researchers all over the world were having similar insights, and over time I became part of a movement for 'participatory action research'.[34] After my PhD, I moved to the University of Bath where I collaborated with colleagues to establish doctoral and masters programmes at the Centre for Action Research in Professional Practice. We thought that research should be a means through which ordinary people could better understand their life situations and learn to act more effectively in their own interests: research *with* people, not *on* people.

This was a radical move, both philosophically and practically. By inviting people to be researchers of their own lives, I had undercut the separation of subject and object at the heart of the western worldview that had been established at the time of the Enlightenment. Francis Bacon urged his fellow seventeenth-century scientists to study nature empirically and establish human dominion over the natural world. The astronomer Galileo Galilei taught that the physical world is open to our gaze if we understand it is written in the language of mathematics, thus emphasizing abstract knowledge over experience. René Descartes' dualism made a radical separation between human and other modes of being. From these developments Isaac Newton formulated his extraordinarily powerful view of the universe as a determinate machine obeying causal laws.[35]

This worldview channels our thinking in significant ways. It tells us the world is made of separate things, that natural objects are composed of inert matter, operating according to causal laws, with no subjectivity or intelligence, no intrinsic purpose or meaning. It tells us that mind and physical reality are separate and that rational abstraction is the way to true knowledge. And it claims that humans, and humans alone, possess mind and subjectivity. The natural conclusion is the belief that it is human destiny and privilege to control, manipulate and benefit from the material resources of the planet. The participative view I was developing offered what Midgley calls 'a different imaginative vision'.

Among the influences on my group of colleagues at the University of Bath was the Polish philosopher Henryk Skolimowski, who was developing the idea of the 'participatory mind'. We invited him to a seminar with our graduate students. Before he arrived he sent an unusual stipulation: that the room we worked in should be one from which we could have access to rocks, trees, water. This was strange, even to me. In the abstract world of university seminars, participation was still what one did with other people. It had nothing to do with the natural world.

Henryk wanted us to develop a sense of deep participation with the natural world.[36] He invited us to go out into the University grounds and identify something with which we wished to engage: a tree or a rock, a natural pool or stream of water, a leaf or a flower. He asked us to calm our minds by sitting quietly, and then to ask permission to engage with our chosen thing; to meditate on its form and presence; to relive its past and its present in our imaginations. He asked us to explore what forms of dialogue were possible. And whether we could find a feeling of identification. At the end he instructed us to disengage, giving thanks for whatever we had received.

To a Northern European it might seem more than a little eccentric, to be invited to talk to trees (the Prince of Wales has never lived it down). But this sense of being part of a living world is deeply rooted in other cultures. My colleague Donna Ladkin wrote about the walks in the woods near Washington she took as a child with her grandfather, a man of Black and Native American ancestry who she called Pepere. On these walks Pepere taught her to talk with trees; not only talk, but to listen to them as well. He would tell her to walk quietly, and say, "See if you can hear the trees talkin' to one another."[37]

• • • • • •

"What I am trying to do on this trip," I explained to Gwen, as we sat in the cabin over the clutter of breakfast, "is to explore this practice of participation more directly. On a long voyage, can I experience a different relationship with the sea and the land?"

I boiled a kettle to wash up, and we tidied away the plates and cutlery in their places, put the milk away under the cabin sole next to the water tank where it would keep cool. Taking the binoculars and camera in a waterproof bag, we went ashore in the dinghy and retraced our steps to the bird hide. There was a new note in the observation book from an early morning birdwatcher: 'female turned round on the nest. Male flew in with some food for her.' We scanned the cliff again, using the magnification of binoculars and telephoto lens to get a closer view; even so it took us ages to spot the nest. The bird was sitting with her back to us, head tucked into a crack in the rock. Her grey and brown markings blended almost perfectly with the patterns on the cliff face, and we could only see her when she turned to preen.

We wandered slowly back along the coast path, enjoying the sunshine and wondering if it really was foggy in the Scillies. On the way we added three more wildflowers to our list – wild geranium, cow parsley (why didn't we see that one before?) and one neither of us could identify.

After a quiet afternoon sitting in the sun we visited St Mawes Castle and had a cream tea in a café on the harbour front. Back on board, the evening forecast was favourable: light easterly winds and no suggestion of fog. After checking the times of the tides we decided to be on our way by seven in the morning to catch the best of the tide around the Lizard and on to the Scillies. With little cloud cover the temperature dropped fast once the sun had gone down, and setting our alarms for six we snuggled under our duvets for an early night.

Chapter Six
Catching the Tide

At a campfire in the Lemhi Range of east central Idaho with Tom Birch and Anthony Weston, Anthony asked, "Why do we go into the wilderness?" After a thoughtful pause, Tom replied, "Wilderness treats me like a human being." Tom's response has been with me for a long time. It is a Zen koan with endless depth, and I keep coming back to it from different angles.
Jim Cheney, *Truth, Knowledge, and the Wild World*[38]

We hauled up the anchor and were out past St Mawes Castle and Black Rock at the entrance to Carrick Roads well before seven. Few people were stirring so early: we passed a couple of inshore fishing boats on their way to check their lobster pots, and the first of the ferries from Falmouth to St Mawes, its wake leaving a trail of ripples on the still water. There was no wind until we reached the Manacles buoy – we passed close by and watched it rock in the slight swell, occasionally giving a mournful clang as it tipped far enough for the clapper to hit the bell. Then we felt a tiny wind on our faces, from the east as forecast, ruffling the sea and just filling the sails, allowing Coral to ghost along on a broad reach.

A 'reach' is the point of sailing where the wind is blowing directly across the boat. On a 'beam reach' the boat is sailing at right angles to the wind, which is blowing across the beam, or width, of the boat. When the wind comes forward of the beam the boat is on a 'close reach'; when it comes more from astern, abaft the beam over the quarter – the side of the boat toward the stern – the boat is on a 'broad' or a 'quartering reach'. For most boats reaching is the fastest and most comfortable point of sailing: the sails form deep aerofoil curves and pull strongly, the boat traverses the direction of the waves, swooping over them rather than into and through them.

In this light wind Coral moved forward pleasantly enough, but at around three knots too slow for us to catch the tide all the way to the Scillies. We needed more power, and I decided to set the spinnaker.

The spinnaker is the big lightweight sail that balloons out in front of a yacht and gives a significant lift when the wind is coming anywhere from just aft of the beam. It is a complex sail, set on its own boom with lots of lines to control it – sheets and guys, uphauls and downhauls. I rarely use it when sailing on my own, but with two of us we could manage it well. It would give us the extra speed for the long sail to the Scillies.

The trick with the spinnaker is to pack it in its bag with no tangles, so it opens cleanly to the wind when hoisted. This time I was out of luck: the sail twisted into an hourglass shape as it went up and I struggled, hauling and releasing on one rope then another, until it decided to untangle itself and set properly. It curved in a great arc down the lee side, catching every drop of wind. Coral heeled over, seemed to gather herself together, and picked up to around five knots. Gwen steered carefully – her first time with a spinnaker flying – as it takes a delicate touch to keep the big sail exactly full of wind. We made good time to past Black Head and out beyond the Lizard.

The sailing directions recommend passing at least three miles to seaward of the Lizard to avoid the rough water and overfalls that can develop close to the headland – and I know from bitter experience how rough the sea can get close in. So we held a southerly course until we were well out to sea, and then turned west, letting the mainsail right out and setting the spinnaker so it bellied out over the bows, to sail directly downwind past Land's End and Wolf Rock toward the Scillies.

Sailing downwind is a delicate business. The plain sails – mainsail and genoa – no longer form aerofoils that suck the boat forward as when close-hauled or reaching. The wind just pushes against them. The sail plan is not stable and balanced, so the boat can easily wander off course. This can result in an accidental gybe, when the wind gets the wrong side of the mainsail and flips it across the boat – irritating rather than dangerous in these light conditions. As the spinnaker is designed for downwind sailing, it gave us a good lift and stabilized the rig. Nevertheless, Aries was not accurate enough, so we had to steer by hand.

Even though we passed well to seaward of the Lizard, the tidal stream was strong and the water disturbed, swirling around and making eddies in the otherwise calm surface even three miles offshore. The white twin towers and cottages of the lighthouse were just visible through the haze, but beyond the Lizard the coast turned north into the big sweep of Mount's Bay and was lost in the mist. Soon the Lizard light faded in turn. Coral was carried west by wind and tide, nearly two knots of tide adding to five knots through the water. We were now making excellent time.

A couple of hours later, as the day warmed up and the mist lifted, the far side of Mount's Bay came into view. Beyond, we caught our first glimpse of the lighthouse on Wolf Rock, a dangerous reef some seven miles southwest of Land's End. As we approached we realized the tide, racing around the end of Cornwall, was setting Coral toward the rock: we had to steer a more southerly course to keep clear. Even a mile to the south, Coral was heaved around as the turbulence in the water caught her keel. There was a quite remarkable strength of tide, well beyond anything I had experienced before in open water. Although far offshore, we could see and feel the mass of water rushing out of the Channel and into the Celtic Sea.

Past Wolf Rock we were out of coastal waters and exposed to the Atlantic proper. As Land's End faded into the mist behind us we were now clearly 'at sea', no longer following the coast but steering a compass course toward the Scillies, in that strange world where there was nothing but the ship in the middle of a vast circle of water and the dome of the sky. This was our first encounter with the wilderness of the ocean.

• • • • • • •

This first encounter with the ocean reminded me of the koan, 'Wilderness treats me like a human being.' A *koan* is part of Chan and Zen Buddhist[39] practice, a paradoxical puzzle, story or dialogue that cannot be resolved by the rational mind. Traditionally, koans are stories of encounters between students and masters; but they can also arise from everyday life. The paradoxical nature of a koan means investigation of their meaning can liberate the mind and shock it into awareness of its constructed nature. It can startle you into seeing how the plumbing of the mind is constructed.

Remembering this koan took me back to my five-day retreat earlier in the year at Winterhead Hill Farm in the Mendips, the house of my friend and Buddhist teacher John Crook. I wanted to explore how meditation practice in the Chan tradition might show me a way toward a practice of participation and the question I was carrying on this voyage: how might I learn to be fully part of the world, to meet it as a community of mysterious subjects rather than as a collection of objects?[40]

The Buddha taught that life is characterised by suffering caused by attachment to a transitory world, and above all attachment to an illusory sense of a permanent self. This illusion of separateness and permanence is one way we stop ourselves participating in enchantment. A period of intensive meditation practice might help to loosen my bonds of attachment to 'Peter' as a separate entity, and through this offer access to the world as participant, rather than as an observer.

Winterhead is a rambling farmhouse on the edge of the Mendips. I arrived on a cold and frosty January afternoon. John showed me the rooms he had set aside for retreats – a bedroom, sitting room and kitchen, and the Buddha room for meditation. Once I had settled in, we sat together at the table in John's kitchen over a cup of tea to talk through how I would spend my time. John first came across Chinese Buddhism as a National Service Officer in Hong Kong immediately after the Second World War.[41] After an academic career as an evolutionary psychologist, he pursued an intensive study of Chan under the guidance of the late Master Sheng-yen[42] in what John called "the work of his retirement".

I looked at John across the table. I thought, as I often do, that he must have been dangerously handsome as a young man. Still tall and slender, he had a full head of brown hair that flopped over his forehead and unruly eyebrows, in complete disregard for style. Strongly featured, his face now carried the evidence of decades of experience and adventuring, his hazel brown eyes peering out quisitively through wrinkles. He was, until his mid-seventies, leading expeditions into the Himalayas, but recently a trapped nerve in his back had made him unsteady on his feet.

I had known John for many years both as personal friend and teacher (we seemed to negotiate these two aspects of our relationship well). He lived alone in his remote farmhouse and liked his own company – although he was personally assertive he could be quite shy – but appreciated friendship and convivial company. Over many years I learned he was profoundly kind, sometimes quite prickly when challenged, and always engaging.

John and I agreed the following simple routine: I would sit in meditation for two thirty-minute sessions, with a brief stretch in between, four times each day: before breakfast, late morning, late afternoon, and in the evening before bedtime. Between these sessions I would take walks around the garden and further afield in the Mendips, walks in which I would attempt to maintain a meditative quality of attention. John agreed to talk with me about my experiences from time to time. I would make occasional audio and written notes. The rest of my time I would spend doing little jobs for John around the house, preparing and clearing up my meals, and sleeping.

I started my retreat by focussing on becoming fully present – leaving behind all the activities of my everyday life and calming my mind, the starting point of most meditation practices.[43] Like many people, I am always busy with thinking and feeling, reflecting on and planning about my business in the world. However worthy this may be in its own right, the Buddha taught that this busy mind is also devoted to establishing and maintaining our self-image and the illusion of our separateness.

I didn't find it easy to slip into meditation practice. It was a struggle to establish the alert yet relaxed posture – even using a meditation stool my knees and ankles felt bent out of shape. As I focussed on my breath, noticing the inhale and the exhale and the pause between them, my mind wandered around, running off into distractions – what was the best recipe for the leek and potato soup I wanted to make for lunch? would it be cold for my walk outside? how should I mend the chair John had asked me to attend to?

Meditation teachers tell us that distraction and wandering thoughts are ever-present; as emotional barriers are lowered the practitioner may also need to confront buried distress and the unfinished business of earlier life. When I mentioned my wandering mind to John, he laughed kindly, reminding me again how common this is. The skill, which is gradually learned and re-learned, is to gently bring attention back to the breath and over time discover an experience of quiet being. This process of calming the mind is common to many meditation practices.

By the afternoon of the second day I had established quite long periods of quiet mind, and went out for a walk. Clambering over the stile, I followed a farm track across a field, and climbed toward the ancient Callow Drove along the ridge above me. Sheep were grazing on grass still frosted where the winter sun hadn't reached. A heavy tractor had left deep grooves in the frozen mud, hatched with the marks of coarse tyre treads. Beyond the field, the path became more rugged as it climbed steeply through neglected coppiced woodland, rough rocks slipping under my feet. Breathing the frosty air deeply, about halfway up I paused for breath and looked around.

My eye caught a movement – brown – to my left. I turned to see a hawk flying in the woods. Bigger than a kestrel, smaller than a buzzard, brown-backed, agile: a sparrowhawk. Effortlessly navigating the narrow gaps between the trees, she was flying quite slowly, probably hunting. She made a tight circle toward me and then was away, back down the hill in a wide arc over the path. Part of me flew off with her and then returned.

Would I have even seen the hawk, brown melding into the fawns and greys of the woodland, if my mind had not been quiet? Would the hawk have even come so close to a busy mind? Did it matter? It was and is a gift, spellbinding, to see a wild bird so close, simply doing her own thing for her own purposes. I continued my walk up the hill.

The point of Chan practice is not only to calm the mind but also to radically confront the illusion of a separate self. Once a degree of calm is established, the Chan method is to open oneself to the presence of the whole body in its wider context. This is 'silent illumination' through which, with time and practice, one can develop into a relaxed 'one point' experience, "present in the presence of the present" as John put it. I am simply here, at ease with myself and with my surroundings, noticing the world as it arises around me. From this place of 'self at ease' the quality of mind begins to change, and experiences of spaciousness, of timelessness, of bliss may spontaneously arise.

On the third day the weather was bright, and I tried meditating outside, looking over the fields toward a small wooded area. It was not easy to sit comfortably, but I nevertheless found it calming and quiet. A shower of rain passed through, not really enough to wet me: I just heard its delicate pattering on the leaves. Then the sun slipped out from behind a cloud, and suddenly I was wonderfully warm. Looking over the field I could see drops of water from the rain hanging on blades of grass, glistening in the sunshine. And with the warmth of the sun came a feeling of movement in the air. It was as if I was directly experiencing the power of the sun to drive the cycles of life – and why was it 'as if'? I *was* at that moment directly feeling it in my own warming up.

Then the clouds came over the sun and everything was cold again. Looking up at the clouds shading us, I remembered that as they shade the Earth they reflect the sun, part of the albedo effect that keeps the atmosphere cool.[44] I realized how we are usually aware of only part of the total arc of the climate system. We may be irritated on this winter's day that the cloud obscures the sun, but don't see that in the larger cycle this is keeping Earth cool so that it remains habitable for animals like us. It is so easy to grumble about the wind or the rain, rather than seeing it as part of a cycle of weather.

What did it take to see myself as part of a wider cycle? I suspect that quietening the mind allowed some clarity: I had become less attached to immediate concerns and purposes, which narrow vision, narrow understanding, narrow what we can experience. With a more spacious mind I was more open to experience the wider system.

As my retreat continued I grew to appreciate the contrast between sitting in the Buddha room and walks outside in the January cold. The Buddha room was small and bright, with windows on three sides. John had filled it with the iconography of Chan and Tibetan Buddhism: an altar with a small statue of the Buddha, another of Avalokiteśvara, the Bodhisattva of loving kindness; on the walls silk drawings from Buddhist mythology; in one corner an almost lifesize Buddha, brightly painted and bedecked with a Tibetan ceremonial scarf; in the opposite corner a large Tibetan drum. At the start of each session I lit a candle and an incense stick on the altar and bowed in respect to the Buddha and the teachings – about as much ceremony as my Nonconformist background would easily accept. But the incense and the images served as reminders of why I was there, and each time I entered the room they drew me more profoundly into meditative practice.

The following day my experiences deepened. I had been sitting quietly using silent illumination and total body awareness. In time I became quite still, watching the movement of breath and body with a few thoughts trickling through the back of my mind but none staying attached. Following Chan practice, I opened my attention to my wider context. Immediately, without any volition or intention or expectation, I found myself in unbelievably extended space: one wide sweep of awareness took in the universe as a whole. In place of my everyday experience of perceiving from the centre of my embodied self, I was an indescribably minute being in the vast, vast reaches of a space that was in some sense alive. I was a speck within this whole, experiencing my tininess. At the same time, I was clearly part of it all, part of a whole that was looking at and comprehending itself in some way. It was as if the universe itself, rather than I, was doing the meditating. It left me feeling giddy.

On reflection, my sceptical self wonders about the veracity of this account. "Is it not odd," I say to myself, "that you created the kind of experience of being part of the whole that you are seeking to articulate? Is this not just fulfilling your expectations?" And yet, and yet, while I can describe what happened in terms of my ideas, the experience itself took me completely by surprise and had its own authenticity: I had no idea that at that moment I would be catapulted into a space that was itself meditating.

The following day I stepped over the rather fragile stile that led from John's garden into the field, and walked through the gap in the straggling hedge down toward the main track. The land dipped down into a hollow where there is a trough for cows to drink at. Nothing special, just a field in Somerset. Beyond the track, part of the West Mendip Way, the land rose again. I could see across to the path through the woods where I met the sparrowhawk.

As I walked down into the hollow, I was again overtaken by this sense of spaciousness. I was no longer a point of consciousness making my way through the world, no longer centred within my skull or my body. It was as if I was extended into the space, reaching out into a vastness around me as that vastness – a space undefined and unlimited – was reaching to envelop me.

I carried on over another stile and across the track. I had to pick my way over the deep ruts full of crazed and opaque ice and through mud churned up by tractor wheels, some places squidgy, other places frozen solid where the sun hadn't struck it. I followed the footpath up the steep climb toward the ridge.

It was as I climbed that 'wilderness treats me like a human being' sprang into my mind with a new meaning. It was such a strange thought! And how odd to think I was in a wilderness, on that muddy churned-up track with barbed wire fences and rusty farm implements lying around. But in this experience of vast spaciousness I felt placed in the wilderness of the wild universe as well as the more tamed countryside of the sparrowhawk's wood. For a few moments I experienced directly the meaning of the koan. This is exactly what it is to be a human being: both a separate self and integral with a greater being witnessing itself; both tiny and part of everything.

At the top of the hill I reached the Callow Drove, turned along it, and walked for nearly two hours. The drove runs straight along the ridge between two lines of stone walls that separate it from the farmed fields. The walls are in places tumbled down, windblown hawthorn and oak growing amongst the scattered stone. At the end of the ridge the path descends sharply through open woodland. As I followed the path I watched the tiny birds flocking in the trees, somehow surviving this long cold winter. Lots of crows were milling around; I heard the occasional harsh call of ravens passing and the mewing of buzzards high above. I kept an eye out for the sparrowhawk, but of course she didn't appear again. At the bottom the path rejoins the West Mendip Way, and I turned right to make a circular walk.

Once again I used my breathing to fill my body with awareness. I found myself again, in that curious way, inhabiting space more thoroughly. I could feel the mud squidging under my feet, the sweat coming through my long johns, the physical weariness from the walk. But I also felt my awareness reach out, so that when I heard the buzzard call it wasn't calling from outside me, but from within the same space – almost the same body – that the buzzard and I inhabited together.

Two walkers came down the hill toward me, maps in hand, picking their way along the rutted track, their boots and gaiters splashed with mud. Embarrassed to be standing there as if in another world, I was about to flip back into being a socialized person again when a blackbird flew past, again in the same curious open space as me.

The walkers came closer, and we exchanged formal greetings.

"Lovely day for a walk, so long as it stays dry."

"It gets very muddy further down the track."

······

Gwen had clearly got the hang of steering Coral downwind with the spinnaker. I went below to the chart table, read our position from the GPS and marked it on the chart with a little triangle, with time, distance travelled and course pencilled alongside. I always keep a regular plot on the chart in case the GPS goes down and I have to navigate by dead reckoning, the traditional pilotage process. Starting from a known point, you measure off course and distance covered, and calculate allowances for the effect of tides using information from tidal charts: 5 nautical miles, course 95°, tidal offset 0.5 nautical miles 185°; draw two lines with the protractor and plot the position. A line of pencil triangles advances across the Admiralty chart toward one's destination. Of course there is quite a bit of skill and judgment required in dead reckoning; but when we first started sailing we piloted across to France that way.

Having plotted our position I checked Coral's current course on the compass and GPS, and saw that the stream was no longer hurrying us on our way to the Scillies, but pushing us northwards. I told Gwen to steer 10° more southerly to offset this.

"Sandwich for lunch?" I asked. With the spinnaker pulling Coral along smoothly and level, it was no trouble to get out the bread, cheese and salad and make one up. As I did so, I wondered at how I had forgotten the significance of those retreat experiences. They were so vivid at the time, but then driven out of mind by everyday practicalities. Now, in the wildness of this stretch of ocean, I was reminded of that strange sense of spacious belonging.

We sailed on through the afternoon, taking turns at the helm. The light easterly wind held up, so we kept the spinnaker flying, powering us along all through the day. Toward the end of the afternoon we began to be impatient for the Scilly Islands to come into sight. The plots on the small-scale passage chart seemed to indicate we were close, but the low-lying islands merged into the misty horizon. Then suddenly there they were, making us wonder how we missed them before. We took the spinnaker down in good time, found the navigation marks for the passage between Gugh and St Mary's, turned into the harbour at Hugh Town, and picked up one of the many visitors' buoys that were vacant.

Chapter Seven
Scillies and Gaia

Our own interest lay in relationships of animal to animal. If one observes, in this relational sense, it becomes apparent that species are only commas in a sentence, that each species is at once the base and the point of a pyramid. All life is relational [...] And then not only the meaning but the feeling about species grows misty. One merges into another, groups melt into ecological groups until the time when what we know as life meets and enters what we think of as non-life: barnacle and rock, rock and earth, earth and tree, tree and rain and air. And the units nestle into the whole and are inseparable from it [....][All] things are one, and one thing is all things [...] It is advisable to look from the tide pool to the stars, and then back to the tide pool again.
John Steinbeck, *The Log from the Sea of Cortez*[45]

S t Mary's harbour was busy with local craft and tourist boats, so next morning, after buying fresh provisions, we decided to move somewhere quieter. We left the mooring and motored across the St Mary's Sound toward St Agnes, the smallest of the inhabited islands in the Scillies, in the southwest of the archipelago. There are several shallow and rocky patches in the Sound, and the pilot book recommends following leading lines and transits between rocks, headlands and prominent features on land. This is usually straightforward, but although it was a fine and sunny day, a light haze blurred the details of the coast so the more distant marks were difficult to pick out. And with this exceptional spring tide, the water level was so low that some of the rocks making up the leading lines were obscured behind islands. We went cautiously.

St Agnes is connected to the adjacent island Gugh to the north by a sandbar that covers only at high tides, creating small sheltered bays on each side. The Cove on the eastern side is pretty and quiet, and usually favoured by visiting yachts, but today it was open to the wind. We made our way to the more sheltered western bay where the tourist boats stop alongside the pier to let their passengers disembark. Sounding our way in carefully, we anchored as far into the bay as the shallow water would allow.

I am particularly fond of St Agnes. It is low lying, just a mile across, and incredibly quiet. Despite the continual influx of tourists, it does feel as if there is a genuine community here. The other Scilly islands were connected in prehistoric times when sea levels were lower, and even today it is possible to wade between some of them at low spring tides. But surrounded by deeper water, St Agnes has been separated much longer.

We landed on the sandy beach next to the jetty and walked inland, past houses nestled into hollows out of the way of the elements and skirting tiny fields with high hedges to provide extra protection from the wind. All were intensively cultivated, some showing the remains of the spring flower crop, now harvested; others with early vegetables poking through the soil. We followed the coastal path, winding past the sandbar and along the side of the Cove. Past the beach the path led onto open heath overlooking the sea. Scrubby heather seemed to be scarcely holding its own in the thin soil; gorse lay low on the ground but was nevertheless blooming golden yellow. Nothing gets to any height in this windswept place.

We walked between vast granite boulders, cracked and sculpted into curious shapes by ages of weathering. We amused ourselves by fantasizing about the shapes: this one a dragon, that a bear, over there a Henry Moore Mother and Child. Gwen leapt lightheartedly onto a low rock and stood where its end cantilevered above the ground, gazing out to sea, her hair blowing back in the fresh wind. One formation in particular caught my attention: two smoothly rounded mounds of granite reminded me of the pelvis and bottom of the famous Neolithic Venus of Willendorf on a much larger scale. The grey rock was richly patterned with lichen – a dark green that was almost black, a soft olive, and a startlingly bright orange. Nestled between the mounds, as in the vulva of the goddess, I noticed a shallow pit where multicoloured granite granules had collected. I remembered when my good friend Stephan Harding picked up a handful of granules just like these, held them out in front of me, and said, "You realize these rocks are participating in life on Earth!"

· · · · · · ·

I had developed a long collaboration with Stephan, who is resident ecologist at Schumacher College in Devon, as part of my work at the University of Bath. Every September for ten years we took our Masters students there for a week-long workshop that explored the natural ecology of the planet.

Stephan was formally trained as a scientific ecologist with an Oxford doctorate and has contributed to the development of Gaia theory, working with its originator, the independent scientist James Lovelock and his early collaborator, biologist Lynn Margulis. He is an extraordinarily effective teacher. I have watched him many times on field trips standing, often in the rain, in his waterproofs and boots, blue woolly hat pulled over his ears, leaning lightly on his thumbstick. He would gather the group together, look around eagerly to engage their attention, and launch into words that leaped between the latest discoveries of science and the mystery of the Earth as a living being. Neither took priority: facts, figures and theories were expressed in the context of love for the living planet. In the classroom he expresses scientific ideas graphically so that the least scientifically literate person can follow them. At times he uses his whole body to re-enact the drama of chemical elements joining into new molecular forms.

Stephan teaches Gaia theory as a fully testable scientific theory and as a reaffirmation of the ancient idea of *anima mundi*, the soul of the Earth. This is a modern articulation of the insight expressed in the 1890s by Alfred Russel Wallace, who is acknowledged as a co-progenitor of Charles Darwin in the theory of evolution by natural selection. Wallace's observations drew him to see the natural world not as 'nature red in tooth and claw', but as complex relations and mutual interdependence. He described the ever-changing Earth as 'one grand organic whole'.[46]

Each year Stephan set out the scientific basis of Gaia theory clearly for our students. It has its origins in James Lovelock's study of the contrasting atmospheres of Earth, Mars, and Venus in the 1960s. Lovelock was renowned as an inventor of sensitive scientific instruments. Invited by NASA to develop instruments that might be landed on Mars to detect the existence of life, Lovelock realized that a space mission might not be necessary. Analysis of the light spectrum of Mars and Venus showed that the atmosphere on these planets is near chemical equilibrium, while the atmosphere of Earth, containing lots of active oxygen gas, remains chemically highly active, held far from equilibrium by the processes of life.

The conventional view at the time was that the physical planet provided an independent context in which life on Earth evolved. In contrast, Gaia theory proposes that life profoundly affects the non-living environment, such as the composition of the atmosphere and the presence of water, which then feeds back to influence the entirety of the living world. Life is explained not as random mutations and necessary adaptation, nor in the slogans of the 'selfish gene',[47] but in terms of interdependence, feedback loops, and dynamic equilibrium. In Gaia theory living and non-living things are not rigidly differentiated, but seen as inter-related. Biologist Lynn Margulis taught that Earth's atmosphere and surface sediments are regulated, at least in part, by the activities of more than 30 million different living organisms.[48] This 'tight coupling' between life and non-life results in what Gaia theorists refer to as an 'emergent property': the capacity of the Earth system as a whole to maintain key aspects of the global environment – such as the composition of the atmosphere and global temperature – at levels favourable to life, despite shocks from both within and outside itself.

Gaian scientists describe the Earth as an evolving and self-regulating living whole. A conventional view espouses the 'Goldilocks' perspective that it is a wonderful serendipity that the planet is in the right place in the solar system with the appropriate physical and chemical conditions for life to emerge: 'Not too hot, not too cold, just right!' It is true that an extraordinary combination of astrophysical and geological circumstances has allowed life to evolve and flourish.[49] But the life on Earth is not just the result of fortunate positioning in the solar system – it isn't simply *in* a habitable zone but is also *making* a habitable zone. Very early on in the history of life on Earth living biota and non-living matter became entangled as a single entity. Life on Earth found a way – photosynthesis – to capture the vast energy of sunlight and use it to make Earth ever more suitable for complex living beings.[50]

The Gaia hypothesis has been tested both empirically and in computer modelling. While Lovelock's original proposal in the 1970s became mired in scientific controversy, it has since become the foundation for scientific understanding of the dynamics of planetary change and stability, sometimes under the less controversial name of 'Earth systems science'.[51]

Stephan remains a scientist. He studies and publishes in academic journals, is skilled as a field ecologist and able to work with computer models of the Earth system. But during his time at Schumacher College he has grown critical of the reductionist and mechanistic worldview of modern times – the worldview Professor Grundy challenged me to explore. Stephan is appalled by the major flaw in this perspective. It leads humans to believe that the whole of nature, including the Earth and all her more-than-human inhabitants, is no more than a dead machine to be exploited as we wish for our own benefit. Over the years I watched him teach I also saw him gain the confidence to reclaim the ancient idea of animism and come to see the Earth as alive, 'a vast sentient presence'. Stephan speaks of chemical elements not as non-living entities, but as participatory beings with characters who interact with each other to form new identities – molecules – with different characters. He traces the idea of *anima mundi* back to Plato, through philosophers such as Spinoza and Whitehead, believing that there has always been a holistic, integrative strand in Western culture, buried beneath the reductionist mainstream.[52]

For Stephan, the most important thing is for people to experience this shift in perspective. Only partly in jest, he suggests that with the emergence of the Gaia perspective, *anima mundi* is now 'stalking' humanity, seeking those who are ready to see the world as a living presence again. Through new understandings and experiences people suddenly 'get it', are 'Gaia-ed', and experience the world in a totally different way.

Gwen had been a student on our Masters programme, so I called her over and showed her the granite granules. We reminisced about our stay at Schumacher College and our walk down the Dart, about Stephan's passion for wilderness, and how he saw Dartmoor as a tragic landscape because it has been denuded of trees. I picked up a handful of granules and let them run through my fingers. "Do you remember Stephan talking about granite as part of the carbon cycle?" I asked.

• • • • • • •

The River Dart thundered down from the moor toward the sea. It was full after recent heavy rain, the water so high that it lapped over the banks, swirling around the roots of trees and making soggy patches in the grass. In dryer weather the water rushes between the rocks scattered across the riverbed in little cataracts, but on that day it poured over the top of them in smooth torrents, pounding into the pools below with a deep roar. We had to shout to hear each other over the noise.

We stopped to inspect a chunk of granite that stuck out from the ground by the side of the path with a green luxuriance of moss growing over the top and hanging down each side. Its surface was pitted like a sugar lump, light grey decorated with patches of black lichen. Embedded fragments of quartz, harder than the surrounding rock, protruded slightly and sparkled in the dappled sunlight. A deep fissure ran vertically down the front face of the granite; over time the crack had filled with organic debris marking a dark line, dividing the surface into two planes. The rock leant back into the bank, surrounded by young bramble shoots and bracken with its rear side underground and hidden from our view. Its shape was evocative. A face kept peering out, suggesting itself to me: the fissure, a nose; two blobs of lichen formed eyes; the moss a head of hair. A troll, maybe?

But granite is alive in a more fundamental sense. This rock had broken off from the dome of granite that erupted from deep in the Earth some 300 million years ago to form Dartmoor. The pitted surface and the fissure down the middle were signs of weathering over geological time. It had been tumbled down the valley. Rain had washed over it. Ice had fractured it. The roots of the moss now found their way into hairline cracks, forcing it further apart physically, and secreting acids that helped break it up chemically. As the rock fragmented, exposing new areas to the rain, it gradually dissolved: carbon dioxide from the atmosphere split calcium from the silicate in the granite and combined with it to wash away in a chalk solution, calcium bicarbonate. Some of this we could see, some we knew from our classroom studies prior to the field trip.

I looked around. Everything in the woodlands along the banks of the Dart was part of this process of turning granite into chalk. Small rocks and gravel tumbled against each other in the torrent. The trees seeded clouds, brought rain and kept the ground and undergrowth damp. The roots of plants broke up and dissolved the granite. Insects and animals pollinated flowers and transported seeds. Bacteria turned vegetable matter into humus, and fungi grew in symbiosis with the roots of the trees, making nutrients more readily available. The river collected the chalk solution and carried it down to the sea.

Stephan asked us to recollect the rest of the story in our imagination. Once in the sea the chalky water was taken up by tiny creatures called cocolithophores. Along with other animals like crabs and molluscs they precipitated solid chalk to form their hard skeletons. When they died they fell to the bottom of the sea and formed a chalky layer, compressed over time into solid chalk rock. So when we look at the white cliffs of Dover we are actually looking at solidified atmosphere. This is a continual self-regulating process through which the carbon dioxide that is spewed out of volcanoes thousands of miles away is locked up in the geology of the planet.

Carbon dioxide is, of course, one of the greenhouse gases which traps heat. If too little is present in the atmosphere Earth will freeze. Too much, and the planet will heat up. Either way, it will no longer support life as we know it. We learned in the classroom before our walk that plant life accelerates the physical weathering of granite by up to 1000 times. When it's warmer this 'biologically assisted rock weathering' goes faster; when it is cooler, slower. This self-regulating cycle keeps the temperature of the planet at levels suitable for life.

It was at this point that Stephan bent down, scooped up a handful of granite granules from the side of the path, held them out and made his provocative statement that the rocks participate in life on arth. We stared at the fragments – bits of black, shades of grey, white quartz, glistening fragments of mica – and attempted to digest the idea that they were part of the process of life.

Gaia theory draws together the disciplines of biology, physics, chemistry, and geology. It offers a view of the Earth as an interacting process, a co-evolution of living things and their environment. The hard line drawn between living and non-living things becomes blurred: we can see that while the granite we were contemplating is not 'alive' in the same sense as a living animal or plant, it is nevertheless 'participating in life on Earth.'

There has been much empirical research to demonstrate the amazing complexity of links between living beings and ecological stability. Many issues remain controversial, but the scientific debate is open and lively. We may argue as to whether the whole Earth system should be seen as a living being, but through Gaia theory we can appreciate the qualities of Earth as a 'system of life' in which all living beings participate.

There is a wonder nestled in all this scientific understanding that can evoke a spiritual response, a sense of sacredness immanent in the whole. Embracing Gaia evokes feelings of amazement at the mystery of it all with no need for belief in a transcendental designer god. As John Steinbeck pointed out, long before Gaia theory was conceived, the religious or mystical response is rooted in an understanding that the human is inextricably related to all reality, known and unknowable.[53]

• • • • • • •

What I had seen along the river Dart was happening here on St Agnes. These patches of granite granules were evidence of how the sea and the plant life – even though so much less vigorous than along the Dart – combine to break down the granite and make its calcium available to join with the carbon in the atmosphere. And the shellfish that the local fishermen catch in their pots are drawing on the calcium carbonate to make their protective shells.

Gwen and I made our way back to the bay where Coral was anchored. The world seemed very alive and vibrant. "The air has a lucent quality," Gwen commented, "it makes all the colours appear so pure, not greyed-out as they were in the mist when we left Plymouth." We played our game of finding names for the colours: the sky was azure blue, the sea bright turquoise in the sandy shallows, shading to dark navy blue as it deepened. But we also remembered we had left Coral anchored in shallow water with a rising tide, so we hurried back and were relieved to see that she was safely where we left her.

The pub garden next to the pier was busy with tourists who had arrived by boat from St Mary's. Seeing a notice offering local ice cream, we went into the bar to treat ourselves. The landlady was apologetic, almost distraught, that she had sold out. "It's the lovely weather," she told us anxiously, as if we were going to be cross. "It's OK," I said, "we won't throw a hissy fit on the floor here." She laughed, but looked relieved. We wondered at this as we walked back to retrieve the dinghy: maybe some visitors are really difficult. "It must be a labour of love to live here," Gwen reflected, "really hard work keeping those fields so lush and productive. And then you have to be nice to tourists as well."

Before we left, I picked up two granite pebbles – one white, one pinkish – to match the one I had collected on Île d'Ouessant off the northwest corner of France a few years earlier, another reminder that 'From Ushant to Scillies 'tis forty-five leagues' – Ouessant was anglicized as Ushant by British sailors contemptuous of French pronunciation. We dragged the dinghy across the sand into the sparkling clear water, and the outboard buzzed us back to Coral. The tide had risen considerably, changing the whole appearance of the bay: we could now see over the sandbar to the open sea beyond. After tea and cake on board as a substitute for ice cream, we pulled up the anchor and made for New Grimsby Sound, between the larger islands of Tresco and Bryher.

Tresco flats, a sandbar that is practically dry at low water, divides New Grimsby Sound from St Mary's Sound. As it was now past half tide, we negotiated the passage over the flats with no problem, and picked up one of the visitors' buoys laid by the Tresco Estate. When I first visited the Scillies there were no buoys laid down in New Grimsby Sound – one was expected to anchor. Then the Estate laid a handful outside the drying harbour; now they cover a large expanse of the sound. It's an echo of the historical enclosure of common space – once you could anchor for free, now you must pay £20 a night for a buoy if you want a sheltered spot.

Soon after we arrived Gwen started frying leeks and garlic for our evening meal. Four men passed by in a dinghy. "Wonderful smell," they called out, "we'll be back for supper!" The tide was running fast through the Sound, giving Coral a hint of a bow wave even while at anchor. Inshore fishing boats hurried back over the flats to St Mary's. As usual we were in our bunks early and fell asleep by nine.

• • • • • • •

I woke early and lay in my bunk for a while, watching the patterns of light on the cabin ceiling moving gently up and down, to and fro, as Coral rocked and turned on the buoy. Gwen slept longer. I got up quietly and climbed outside.

It was a beautiful day; weak April sun breaking through thin high cloud. I felt a light wind from the east or northeast, confirming the forecast for northeasterly winds Force 4. Ideal for the crossing to Ireland. I could see past Cromwell's Castle to the sea beyond, north and west toward Kinsale. It looked inviting. In the opposite direction were the twin peaks of uninhabited Samson and in the further distance St Mary's was just emerging through the haze. Tresco was silhouetted by the low sun while Bryher on the far side of the Sound was brightly lit, its golden gorse, white houses and the yellow line of the beach vibrating against the greens, browns and greys of fields and rocks. While I waited for Gwen to wake up I followed my feelings about the trip so far. I was still full of uncertainties and doubts. I found myself wondering again if journeys such as this one were like meditational retreats – it usually takes a while to 'arrive' to let go of the worries and pre-occupations and settle into the experience.

Over breakfast we decided to leave for Kinsale after an early lunch. We would sail through the Celtic Sea overnight and arrive in daylight. This gave us a few hours to explore a bit of Tresco and buy some fresh food for the crossing, so we went ashore in the dinghy.

Tresco is very much a holiday island. Two miles long, and no more than a mile at its widest, the northern end is rough hillside and moorland, while the soft centre and south are developed. We took the road over the centre of the island toward Old Grimsby. We remarked how the old four-square granite houses were restored to perfection, their paintwork clean and bright. The hedgerows and grass banks were carefully managed, trimmed back to neat grass or allowed to grow just long enough for white bluebells and wildflowers to flourish. The farm gates and stiles all looked new or in prime condition, properly fastened with latches in good order – not a glimpse of bailer twine in sight! There were wastebins everywhere, tastefully concealed behind wooden palings and marked for recycling different materials. No cars are permitted on Tresco, so there were only Estate employees going about their business in tractors and electric buggies, waving cheery greetings as they passed.

We followed the gentle rise in the road to the centre of the island, and over the low crest to St Nicholas church, ancient-looking but actually Victorian Gothic, standing in a churchyard full of crumbling gravestones.

Past the church we caught sight of a cow suckling her calf in the corner of a field full of wildflowers. Further on we came to Old Grimsby harbour, which looks out over rocks and islets toward St Martin's, Round Island and St Helen's Pool. It was all tastefully developed, with the Island Hotel on the waterside and timber holiday homes, each with a secluded courtyard, lining the bay. There was little left that appeared 'old' apart from the quay, where visitors stood in an orderly queue waiting for the boat to take them to St Martin's.

It was all very lovely, but we realized that the scene we were walking through – beautiful and peaceful as it was – had been entirely constructed as a pastoral idyll for the benefit of the visitors. Underneath the pastiche we saw hints of an older Tresco. Some of the walls are clearly quite ancient, constructed out of enormous chunks of granite – easy to move with modern fork lift trucks, but a day or more work for a gang of men working with davits and tackle, horse and cart.

Everything seemed so tightly controlled, from the lack of litter to the well-organized visitors to the cheery Estate employees. We wandered back to the New Grimsby side, to yet another expensively tasteful development for the stores, laundry, post office and café. An elderly lady accosted me as I went through the door. "Wonderful what they have here," she exclaimed without any introduction, "much nicer than Tesco!"

"Must be run by Waitrose then," I replied in jest – but of course it wasn't. It is another enterprise of the Estate, full to the brim of the local and the organic and the thoroughly expensive.

As we walked around we wondered to each other if there was something feudal about it all, that Tresco is a benign autocracy where even the visitors are well behaved. What would happen if we stepped out of line? I found it telling that on the wall of the café terrace next to the store, three bright murals proclaimed Peace, Love and Happiness. There were tea towels with reproductions of them for sale inside the store. The original 1960s song, made famous by the rock musical *Hair*, asserted 'Peace, Love, *Freedom*, Happiness'. The 'Freedom' of the song seemed to have disappeared from Tresco.

Was I being too cynical? Probably, in parts at least. But what is the cost in fossil fuels of maintaining this bucolic idyll, I wondered, as I read a note at the newspaper rack in the stores, apologizing for the late arrival of newspapers, which are flown in by helicopter each day. What is the carbon cost of integrating urban expectations into pastoral bliss? While the granite of St Agnes slowly plays its part in the carbon cycle, Tresco shows how we can blithely, without intention and certainly without awareness, pour carbon dioxide into the atmosphere and overwhelm the self-regulation of the Gaian system. The rate of carbon dioxide emissions from human consumption of fossil fuels is in the region of two hundred times that naturally emitted by volcanoes. The visitors come for clean air and peace in pursuit of a good life, yet the fossil fuel based economy that enables them to do so is part of a process that will in time flood these beautiful islands.

And how convenient it all is, you might say, as you watched us return to Coral powered by an outboard, and later motor out of New Grimsby Sound on our way north and west to Ireland. There is no use being smug about it; we are all part of the problem.

Chapter Eight
Across the Celtic Sea

We learn a place and how to visualize spatial relationships, as children, on foot and with imagination. Place and scale of space must be measured against our bodies and their capabilities. A 'mile' was originally a Roman measure of one thousand paces. Automobile and airplane travel teaches us very little that we can easily translate into a perception of space. To know that it takes six months to walk across Turtle Island/North America walking steadily but comfortably every day is to get some grasp of distance [...] I think many of us would consider it quite marvellous if we could set out on foot again, with a little inn or a clean camp available every ten or so miles and no threat from traffic, to travel across a large landscape [...] That's the way to see the world: in our own bodies.
Gary Snyder, *The Practice of the Wild*[54]

We returned to Coral after our walk around Tresco in time for the midday shipping forecast. It confirmed the earlier prediction of moderate winds from east or northeast – coming from the same high-pressure system that had dominated the weather all week. This was ideal for our crossing north and west to Kinsale. With a certain nervous anticipation we got ourselves ready. After lunch we tidied the cabin so that nothing was loose and could fall about in rough seas. We made sure that the food we would need was ready to hand: pasta and pesto sauce for supper, apples, chocolate and biscuits for snacks, porridge for breakfast. We sorted out layers of clothes – it was warm and sunny in the middle of the day, but we knew it would get very cold at night – and put waterproofs and lifejackets where we could get them quickly. Once we were sure everything was ready, we let go of the mooring and motored past the bleak stone walls of Cromwell's Castle, between the broken rocks that reach into the sea at the northern ends of Tresco and Bryher, out of New Grimsby Sound and into the Atlantic Ocean.

The GPS gave us the bearing and distance to Kinsale: 245° and 134 miles.

Coral was sailing comfortably on a reach with Aries set to steer. We sat in the cockpit enjoying the afternoon sun, looking astern from time to time to watch the Scilly Isles disappear. When crossing the Channel to go to France the high land of Dartmoor stays in view for a while, but the low-lying Scillies soon dropped below the horizon.

Even in settled weather like this, it felt bold to sail directly away from the coast and out to sea, knowing that the next land was well over 100 miles away. We were sailing right across the Fastnet sea area, open to the full force of the weather and waves of the Atlantic Ocean. In these early hours, before I had settled fully into the rhythm of the crossing, I fussed around, making sure everything was in order, that the sails were set just so, that I had chosen the right course for the conditions and weather outlook. I didn't really relax until it was clear we had left the Scillies behind and there was nothing but the wide circle of sea around us, the endless waves reaching to the curve of the horizon and the vast bowl of the sky above.

The wind held steady for a while, then dropped back to practically nothing. To our surprise, a tiny brown bird landed on the edge of the cockpit, seeming to arrive from nowhere. It settled for a moment, feathers ruffling in the wind, hopped onto the toe of my boot, then flew under the sprayhood. We tried to give it water but, frightened, it fluttered around in panic and hid under the folds of a chart. Soon it took off and flew away, the wind picked it up and blew it further out to sea. The little bird was completely out of place. We could not imagine it would survive long.

• • • • • • • •

From the perspective of land it is easy to forget the watery extent of the planet. I often wonder how it is that, as an island race, so few British people have this experience of the wildness of the ocean. From where we were sailing there was nothing except ocean to the west between us and North America; south by west nothing until Brazil and beyond that the Antarctic. There is so much water on Earth that we don't usually notice it. Gaia is a thirsty, soaking wet planet, and it is this that makes the atmosphere energetic and reactive compared with the carbon dioxide worlds of Mars and Venus.[55] Water is an extraordinary molecule, appearing in nature as solid, liquid and gas; its particular molecular structure gives it strong attractive forces that create the capillary action essential for vascular plants such as trees. It is fundamental to living things, the solvent that supplies the continuous flow of essential elements. Without water there would be no life; without life, Earth would long ago have lost its water. Sensitivity to water, its quantity and saltiness, may be the most elemental of all senses: rupture the semi-permeable membrane that makes up the external boundary of a cell, whether it be a tiny bacterium or a large egg, and that cell dies, unable to maintain its identity. One might even see life as 'animate water'.[56]

I remember Stephan explaining that the three inner planets, Venus, Earth and Mars had developed in similar ways, and all had water up until about 3,500 million years ago. Both Venus and Mars lost their water by evaporation as they heated up through a combination of solar radiation and local greenhouse effects. In contrast, with the emergence of life some 2,500 million years ago Earth became a Gaian planet, a living ecology in which organisms actively retained water and countered the tendency to desiccation. As Gaia theory shows, living things relate to their environment not by passive adaptation but by 'active fitting'.

Earth is able to retain its wetness through a combination of biological and physical processes. A major challenge is the potential loss of hydrogen, a gas so light that it can reach escape velocity from Earth's gravitational field and dissipate into space. There are many physical and biological processes that might contribute to this. For example, the ferrous oxide in basalt, which makes up the majority of the seabed, can strip oxygen from seawater and integrate it into solid rock. This frees the hydrogen. Countering this, bacteria and algae liberate oxygen through photosynthesis, which is then available to combine with hydrogen, recapturing it as water. This, and other self-regulating processes, maintain Earth as a wet planet. Harding and Margulis suggest that our planet might be better named 'Water' than 'Earth' because of its extent and significance.

Ocean currents contribute to the absorption of carbon dioxide through the global circulation of water. As the sun beats down and warms the water in tropical latitudes, tongues of warm water move toward the high latitudes, for example in the Gulf Stream and North Atlantic Current. The Scilly Isles, the coastline of Cornwall and southwest Ireland, even parts of western Scotland, demonstrate this in their gardens where tropical plants flourish.[57]

As the water travels into colder regions, it loses heat to its surroundings and some evaporates, so by the time it reaches the high latitudes it is dense, colder and very salty. In both the Arctic and Antarctic, where it meets the cold and fresher polar water, it plunges dramatically down, taking huge amounts of carbon with it. These warm surface flows are complemented by cold currents deep underwater that return the water to the tropics.

Gaian scientists liken this vast global flow of water to the flow of blood, distributing heat and nutrients around the planet.

Increasingly, scientific journals are publishing articles on Gaian themes, demonstrating the extraordinarily complex links between living beings and ecological stability. One of my favourites explores the contribution sperm whales make to the efficiency of the carbon pump that buries carbon dioxide deep in the Southern Ocean. Carbon dioxide is directly, physically, soluble in water, but life is still involved. By consuming prey at depth and defecating iron-rich liquid faeces on the surface, sperm whales fertilize and encourage the blooming of phytoplankton. As they grow, the plankton draw carbon dioxide from the atmosphere; and when they die, they sink to the bottom, exporting the carbon to the deep ocean. Geo-engineering enthusiasts propose seeding oceans with iron in order to stimulate this carbon pump: it appears that whales do this naturally and in significant amounts. Industrial whaling has over time reduced the input of iron to the Southern Ocean by 450 tonnes annually, significantly decreasing carbon export to the deep ocean.[58] It would seem we don't need bioengineering so much as more whales: biodiversity plays a key role in climate stability.

Humans began to influence the climate of the planet as soon as they started hunting on a significant scale, killing off the large herbivores that some scientists argue increased ecosystem productivity.[59] Through the history of civilization, the influence of humans on the planet has steadily increased. Now, in the twenty-first century, the impact of human activities in shifting energy and material is on a scale comparable to the natural processes of the planet. The challenge is that this impact is both vast and hidden from human experience. Purely scientific understanding is not sufficient. The poet John Keats put it very well: ideas are of no use until they are 'proved upon our pulses'.

• • • • • • •

The wind picked up again and backed further northeast. We adjusted the sails and Aries to account for the new wind direction, and Coral settled down to a comfortable six knots – about seven miles an hour. If we kept this speed up through the passage we would reach Kinsale in well under thirty hours, sailing through the night and arriving midday tomorrow. We were travelling at about the speed of human running. My neighbours back at home are amazed that when I go on these long sailing trips I take five or six days to sail a distance that could be covered in a couple of hours by plane.

Slowing the pace of travel is important if we want to re-establish a conversation with the world. Gary Snyder writes of listening to an Australian Aboriginal elder telling stories while they drove along a dusty road, sitting back in the bed of a pickup near Alice Springs. He began to speak very rapidly, telling the story of a mountain over there, then another about some wallabies that got into some kind of mischief with lizard girls. Hardly had he finished, than he started on another story about a hill over here and another story over there. Snyder recounts how he couldn't keep up. He realized after about half an hour that these were tales to be told while *walking*, and what he was getting was a sped-up version of what might be leisurely told over several days of foot travel.[60]

Elsewhere, Snyder reflects on the travelling of Buddhist monks in Japan, walking the mountain trails between monasteries – one day to four weeks' walk. He suggests that, like them, we learn to understand spatial relationships through active engagement, measuring place and scale against our bodies and our imagination.[61]

Gwen and I settled down for the long trip, enjoying the sunshine. As evening approached, we tucked ourselves under the sprayhood, out of the wind. My mind moved into a quiet, meditative space induced by the sea and the wind. There was nothing to do except make sure the boat kept sailing well and safely, look out for ships and changes in the weather, plot our position every hour, eat a bit, and sleep as much as we could. We talked together about passage-making. Gwen was rather anxious, very much on alert – it was only her second overnight passage.

"It's not often I do something that takes me so far out of my comfort zone. I like the challenge," she said.

Coral may be a construction of human culture, but she enables, even invites us, to be more intimately linked with the physical world of wind, water and weather. We were measuring the world against our physical capacities and bringing our experience back to its proper scale.

Gwen took the first watch after supper while I went below to sleep. She called me around eleven.

"What's it like up there?" I called up the companionway.

"Cold. Very cold."

I put on layers of warm clothes, starting with long underwear, then fleecy salopettes, scarf and finally my ancient waterproofs. I was wearing so much I had to let out the webbing to get into my lifejacket harness.

Before I went on deck I checked the GPS, read our distance and bearing from a waypoint in the middle of the Celtic Sea, plotted them on the chart with the protractor and drew a triangle to mark our position. Next to it I pencilled the time and distance travelled from the log. Keeping this record every hour is an important safety measure in case the electronic instruments fail, and I like to have a visual sense of where I am on the crossing. I was happy with the line of triangles across the chart: we were making good progress.

As I climbed out of the companionway I clipped my safety line to the strong point in the well of the cockpit – I have a firm rule that no one goes on deck in the night without first attaching a safety line. Stepping from the close confines of the cabin into the immense space of the night I was for a moment disoriented. In the thick darkness I could see almost nothing but the glow of the instruments and the loom of the masthead navigation light swaying with the roll of the boat; we used as little light as possible to preserve our night vision. I peered over the sprayhood, looking around, taking in the vague shapes of the waves, the patterns of clouds, the distant dots of light. Gradually my eyes adapted to the low light.

"Anything about?"

"Quite a few fishing boats." Gwen pointed out the distant lights. "We're passing that group over there. That one over on the horizon to starboard has been in the same place for an hour. And I think the one ahead will pass in front of us, you need to keep an eye on it. I'm frozen."

Gwen went below. I looked around until my eyes had adjusted to the dark and I knew for sure where all the fishing boats were, then climbed back into the cabin to find an apple and a large chunk of chocolate. As I tiptoed past Gwen I saw she had snuggled under her duvet and was breathing regularly: she seemed to have dropped off to sleep straight away. Back on deck, I settled down in the corner of the cockpit, sheltered by the sprayhood and wedged in with my legs braced against the opposite side. Every now and then I stood and looked over the hood to check the position of the fishing boats: as Gwen predicted, one passed well ahead of us, the rest disappeared astern. There is never much traffic in the Celtic Sea, unlike in the English Channel, where one can see twelve or more big ships at a time when crossing the shipping lanes.

It was a murky night. The sea appeared dark, the waves as ill-defined lumps. To the west the line of the horizon was blurred. Directly above, stars shone weakly through thin cloud. In the southeast the sky was lighter, the line of the sea sharper – the moon was somewhere down there below the horizon. The night colours were extraordinary: not pure, not black and white or silver, but definitely colour. It was a gloomy greeny bluey grey, an inky grey.

I sailed on for hours and hours through the darkness, with its indistinct shapes and muted colours. With my primary sense of sight disabled, time and space were distorted. I had a sensation, almost a hallucination, of charging recklessly forever into an unfathomable void, travelling through an empty space – and in a way, of course, we were.

As my watch wore into the small hours, damp cold seeped through my seaboots and my bottom ached against the hard seat. My strange imaginings were amplified by a horrible sense of fatigue. There were moments when I ached with a tiredness that haunted every moment, when my eyes wouldn't stay open, my head kept dropping down and it felt impossible to stay awake. Although deeply unpleasant, all these disorientations are central to the experience of a crossing. They took me out of the everyday, away from all cues as to what to experience.

After a while the sky in the southeast lightened further. The moon had risen, the loom of its light spilling out from behind the clouds which hid it. Then it burst into view, on the wane a few days after full moon, a little hazy, yellowy orange. I chuckled to myself: it really was the colour of a rich cheese. The sea underneath turned metallic, like deep, dark steel. Now the moon had risen the atmosphere of the night changed: shadows appeared and the wind vane above the stern was more precisely silhouetted. The moonlight gave drama and shape to the clouds above, while hiding most of the starlight. It created a powerful contrast between this brightness and detail in the east and the darkness that shrouded the sky in the west behind me.

Looking astern I could see Aries waving gently back and forth, nudging the tiller this way then that to keep Coral on course. There was a slight sea running; Coral was going very fast, leaping over it like a live creature. Water cascading noisily in a phosphorescent wake on the dark sea, a deeper note sounding as the bows dropped into a wave, a lighter arpeggio under the stern as she lifted clear. Every now and again she rolled more to leeward in a gust, then came up again; sometimes she pitched up as a wave hit the bow. It was nothing violent, just a meeting and responding to the force of the winds and the waves.

When Gwen came up later for her watch, she looked around, saying, "The water is so alive. I've been listening down below, and have a sense of it having different moods and reacting with the boat in different ways." Her face lit up in the moonlight as she remembered. "Yesterday afternoon it was soft and caressing and soothing and gentle. During the night the bangs and crashes are more aggressive, busier, angrier... maybe not angry but less comfortable, less loving."

Gwen's watch took us into daylight, but there was still a long way to go. I made porridge for an early breakfast – always comforting after a night of watches. The day remained cold for a while as the sun climbed slowly above the horizon. It became pleasantly warm, then suddenly far too warm. I quickly stripped off my long underwear and in lighter clothes took over from Gwen, who was still cold and retired again under her duvet.

It felt like an age before the Irish coast came into sight, then suddenly the headland – Old Head of Kinsale – appeared, and beyond that the mouth of the river. As we closed the coast a waft of air from the land hit us: warm, humid, carrying the pungent smell of vegetation. We had arrived.

• • • • • • •

I cooked up a big late-morning breakfast – bacon, eggs, toast and coffee – and looked back on the experience of the passage: the sense of vast space in the middle of the big disc of ocean, the strange colours and shapes, the tiredness and weird shifts in consciousness. It was odd that there was not much we could find to say.

"Now we are no longer in it, it's difficult to tell you what it was like," Gwen paused, as if searching her memories, "because words don't seem to work for it really. There's a world of experience that you can't quite grasp when you are out of it."

Hillaire Belloc wrote in his essay *The Idea of Pilgrimage* that an intense experience of the world is only available to those who travel on foot.[62] He clearly hadn't made a night passage in a small yacht. It's a different space, like a dream world, that fades away with the brightness of the day.

Chapter Nine
Kinsale, Baltimore, Dunmanus

There are at least two kinds of games. One could be called finite, the other infinite.
A finite game is played for the purpose of winning, an infinite game for the purpose
of continuing the play...
If a finite game is to be won by someone it must come to a definite end.
Infinite players cannot say when their game began, nor do they care. They do not care
for the reason that their game is not bounded by time. Indeed the only purpose of the
game is to prevent it coming to an end [...] Infinite players [...] continue their game in
the expectation of being surprised. If surprise is no longer possible, all play ceases.
James P. Carse, *Finite and Infinite Games*[63]

It was quiet in Kinsale overnight but by no means silent – we were after all in a substantial town again with a busy port. Early in the morning the hum of cars on the riverside road, the harsh clatter of outboard engines on the river, the metallic bang of hatches on trawlers all stood out as separate sounds. As the town woke to its morning business they merged into one background buzz punctuated by staccato crashes that gradually stirred us from our sleep. Gwen packed her bag, put on shore-going clothes and I took her to the quay in the dinghy. I felt odd and rather sad, leaving her standing forlornly waiting for the bus to Cork Airport.

Now I was on my own. There was a lot to do before I could leave – everything takes much longer single-handed. I bought fresh milk and bread, and made two trips with my plastic containers to fill the water tanks. Back on board, Coral's cabin seemed rather empty, so I moved things around to take possession of the whole space. I hauled up the dinghy, deflated it and lashed it down on the coachroof, stowing the oars and seat in the cockpit locker. I made doubly sure my gear – winch handles, waterproofs, binoculars – was stowed in the proper places so I could quickly lay my hands on what I needed. It was late morning before I was ready to haul up the anchor and motor down the river.

As Coral got underway I felt an anxious and excited thrill. Now it was all up to me: there was just one pair of eyes to look around, one pair of arms to winch the ropes. I moved cautiously about the boat, thinking through each move systematically, keeping a careful eye out for the way Coral drifted in the stream, the position of other boats in the river, the big red buoy that marks the end of the shallow spit. Once the anchor was up, the propeller bit the water and Coral had steerage way, I relaxed a bit and set a course down the river, enjoying the solid feel of the tiller in my hand and the way she responded quickly to a touch of rudder. As I left the river the wide bay opened in front of me. It was a quiet day with little wind and a slight sea, giving me a chance to settle down into my single-handed routine.

The sail west with the tide to Baltimore was long but uneventful. The continuing high pressure brought with it very poor visibility, so that after rounding the Old Head the coastline was lost in the haze, only coming into view as I passed each headland – Seven Heads, Galley Head, Toe Head. Coral pottered along gently, but with the light wind astern I had to steer by hand through much of the day, which was tiring. Then, about ten miles from Baltimore, the wind picked up, clearing away the mist and hurrying Coral along. The late afternoon sun cast a warm light and long shadows, emphasizing the fissures and folds in the rocks of Kedge Island. Lot's Wife, the white beacon high on the cliff at the entrance to Baltimore Harbour, caught the sun, light and shadow emphasizing its elegantly curving shape in delightful contrast to the fractal patterns of the rocks below.

After a day of poor visibility, all this sharp and dramatic detail aroused me. The cliffs seemed to have a presence and to call forth a response. I reached for my notebook and scribbled a few descriptive notes of what I could see, but my emotional response at the end of this tiring, misty day was just, "How wonderful!" Then, through the narrow entrance, I caught sight of the smooth waters of Baltimore Harbour, and I felt invited, welcomed into the shelter. Coral slipped easily between the cliffs and past the green starboard-hand buoy that marks the dangerous Loo Rock lurking underwater in the entrance.

Once through the entrance, the wide expanse of water, sheltered from the sea by Sherkin Island and an arm of the mainland, stretched out calm for about a mile in each direction. On the west coast of Ireland all sheltered bays are called a harbour whether they have any facilities or not. The harbour proper, enclosed by two concrete breakwaters, nestles in the corner of a small bay on the southern shore below where the town of Baltimore clusters up the hillside. The bay was crowded with moorings and the harbour too busy and shallow for Coral, so I picked a spot further out and dropped anchor clear of the fairway.

· · · · · · ·

Next morning when the alarm woke me early for the weather forecast there was damp, even some rain, in the air, quite a change after the weeks of dry weather we had been enjoying. The Irish sea area forecasts are detailed and helpful, although the style and manner of delivery is quite different from the formality of the UK Shipping Forecast with its defined areas and coded information. The BBC announcer reading the forecast script is a distant figure speaking from Broadcasting House. But the lady at Met Éireann had a soft and calm voice; I almost felt she was in the cabin, speaking directly to me, telling me about slow-moving frontal troughs over the west coast. Looking out I saw the low cloud settling over Sherkin Island. The harbour entrance was misty and the northern exit from Baltimore, which follows an intricate route between tiny islands and submerged rocks to Roaringwater Bay, was scarcely visible. There was no point in pushing on through this mist and murk. I decided to stay put for the morning.

I was pleased with myself the previous night, getting all the way from Kinsale, but this change in the weather depressed me somewhat. I was counting on continued easterlies to get me around Mizen Head today. I wanted to get to the Blaskets by the middle of the following week, when the neap tides would make the tricky pilotage around the islands easier. Then I asked myself, "What am I up to? Why the hurry? Why not take things more slowly?"

I went below to make coffee and picked out James Carse's *Finite and Infinite Games* from the bookshelf. I had bought it just before I left home, and hadn't yet read it properly. The most critical distinction between a finite and an infinite game is that the rules of an infinite game change in the course of play, and they change in order to keep the game in play. The rules of an infinite game, wrote Carse, are like the grammar of a living language, always evolving to support creative discourse. "Surely," I told myself as I flicked through the pages, "I am not playing a finite game on this voyage." My journey was best seen as part of an infinite game, the purpose of which was to keep the whole experience in play. It might well be sensible to arrive at the Blaskets at neaps, but it was not an absolute necessity.

I realized how important it was to keep the rules open and the game continuing. My purpose was not to reach the Blaskets, but to play with the possibilities that arose while travelling. I was not trying to win against the wind and weather but rather to engage with them. To do so I must remember Meeker's injunction to keep a clear-eyed and open attention to the present. This didn't mean I might not be ambitious, might not stretch myself and my capabilities. But it did mean I mustn't fix on closed rules that blinded me to wider opportunities.

I took this idea of open, playful awareness into the cockpit with my second cup of coffee to look around. Change was afoot. The cloud was lifting. The air remained damp but it had stopped raining. The hills above Baltimore and on Sherkin Island were still obscured, while the lower lying ground had that soft, just-showing-green-through-the-mist quality that is so characteristic of Ireland. Colours everywhere were muted, and it was quiet except for the low roar of surf on the rocks at the harbour entrance, and a periodic metallic banging from the trawlers moored at the quay. A black-backed gull landed alongside Coral to inspect a piece of paper bobbing in the water. As I turned to watch she flapped her wings, starting to take off, cautious that I might be a threat; but in the midst of her alarm she appeared to decide I was harmless after all and settled back in the water, fussing her feathers into position.

I could see the harbour entrance clearly now and through it to a fuzzy horizon. There was a light wind from the north, enough for sailing. Going below again (sometimes sailing seemed to entail endless clambering up and down the companionway) I looked through the charts. The direct course for Mizen Head lay outside Clear Island; if the weather became unsuitable I would cut north into Crookhaven, the last harbour on the south coast. After Mizen, the next obvious shelter was rather a long way further, on the north side of Bantry Bay at Castletownbere or somewhere in Berehaven. As I looked at the chart again I remembered there is shelter just north of the Mizen in Dunmanus Bay, a narrow finger of water that sweeps thirteen miles east by north. This bay is relatively undeveloped, with only a scattering of settlements. Dunmanus Harbour – about half way up on the southern side – is described as a 'wild and attractive place' in my old pilot book. I didn't need fixed rules: I would hold these alternative destinations in mind and see how the day unfolded.

I made myself a sandwich for lunch and cleared up ready for leaving, checking around the cabin to make sure everything was safely stowed. I tucked Carse's book in with the others in the bookcase, noticing how their corners were already rather dog-eared. My notebook was also soggy at the edges from being left under the sprayhood overnight. Boats are not good places for books, they get wet and crumpled very easily. I started the engine, pulled up the anchor hand over hand, and motored gently into the wind while I hoisted the mainsail. Reversing the track I took coming in last night, I steered to avoid the shallow patches in the harbour, passed through the entrance leaving the Loo Rock buoy close to port and turned west toward Cape Clear Island.

At sea everything felt fresh and clear. My spirits lifted. I had made the right decision to wait until the day woke up properly. I was able to sail past the long curved ridge of Cape Clear Island, just making out two towers against the sky and the heathery seaward-facing slopes, all bluey grey in the haze. Over the port bow, I could see the Fastnet Rock with its steep sides and prominent lighthouse emerging abruptly out of the sea. Further on, where the tidal stream is forced between Cape Clear and the Rock, the sea became choppy and uncomfortable. But once through this exposed stretch it was calm again, the sun came out, and Coral sailed happily across Long Island Bay toward Mizen Head.

Crossing the bay I was entertained by the bird life. An oystercatcher flew across the bows calling loudly, orange beak catching the sunlight. Groups of guillemots bobbed about on the water or flew off, their little wings beating furiously. Gannets passed in low processions, white feathers standing out against the dark sea. They flew so close to the water their wings seemed to catch the tops of the waves, then soared upward a few feet, dropping down again to disappear for a moment behind the light swell. Gulls swooped around Coral, scavenging for food.

Something unusual caught my eye: a brownish bird with powerful wings. It flew upwards and attacked a gull that was ambling around in the sky. The gull evaded once, but the aggressor persisted, catching it by the wing. They tumbled together toward the water, flapping violently. Something dropped; the brown bird let go and chased toward the sea, while the gull flew off, disconsolately, it seemed to me. The brown bird must be a skua, I thought, and checked with the bird book. I read that skuas attack gulls and other seabirds and force them to regurgitate recent meals, which the skuas then eat. I discovered this practice has rather delightfully been termed 'kleptoparasitic'.

With a light heart I sailed on toward Mizen. Maybe it was the sunshine, maybe it was all the wildlife. The moment felt playful: there was nothing to achieve at the moment, no one and nothing to please.

As I closed with the coast details on the land became clearer: a patchwork of fields, a few cows, the occasional house, a radio mast reaching up into the clouds. Beyond these the arch of the bridge reached across to the island that forms the head itself, where a group of white buildings cluster around the lighthouse. Then the wind suddenly died away and I had to start the engine. The sea became more disturbed again as the tide rushed past the Head. The gentleness I had experienced in Long Island Bay was transformed in the space of a quarter, maybe half an hour, into a strong feeling of wildness, of the end of the land, of reaching out into the Atlantic Ocean. I was going around the most southwesterly point of the British Isles. Firm purpose and playfulness had come together.

Clear of Mizen I turned north, skirting the rugged and steep coast for the short distance up to Three Castle Head at the entrance to Dunmanus Bay. This head is a wonderfully complex formation of rocks, the three ruined castles from which it gets its name settled in a high grassy saddle between two peaks. In places the cliffs drop sheer into the water where the rock has split along the line of the strata leaving smooth vertical planes. This stretch of coast was compressed from the south in what is known as the Variscan folding in late Palaeozoic times, folding the rocks like the bellows of an accordion. Over time the upward folds eroded, exposing the lower strata. The sea rose and flooded the valleys created by the downward folds, leaving the pattern we now see: fingers of land reaching into the Atlantic at Cape Clear, Mizen, Sheep's Head, Dursey, Valentia and Dingle. This geological history of the area is directly visible in the twisting patterns and tortured curves of the rock strata of these cliffs.[64]

The wind picked up again, now from the southwest, and I set the sails for a broad reach. I looked over my shoulder into the wind at a darkening and lowering cloud hurrying over the horizon. Another frontal trough moving in from the Atlantic, I thought; that explained the freshening wind after the sudden lull around Mizen. As I sailed past Three Castle Head into the mouth of Dunmanus Bay the high land and steep cliffs gave way to a sheltered hollow where human habitation and cultivation were again possible. The patchy sunshine picked out one of the white houses surrounded by its stony green fields, leaving the rest in shadow. Out of the open sea in the shelter of the bay the water was smooth, but the wind was gusty as it funnelled round the headland. A little squall danced a dark ruffle of turbulence across the surface, picked Coral up and urged her along. Over the land, dark rain clouds sharpened the blue of the sky. Sunlight reappeared for a moment, then serious cloud, heavy with rain, gathered over the peaks. Coral and I were in a race with the weather: would we reach Dunmanus Harbour, about halfway up the bay, before rain and heavy squalls hit us?

Standing in the cockpit, steering with the tiller between my buttocks, I studied the pilot book again. The entrance to Dunmanus Harbour is narrow with sunken rocks on both sides, and there is often a breaker described as 'rather frightening'. But the pilot book told me that, despite appearances, the entrance is straightforward: keep in mid-channel and head just to the west of the ruined castle. I sailed up the bay with heightened anticipation. What would I find there? It was unlikely to be completely deserted. If there were shelter and a place to moor, it would have been used by fishing boats for hundreds, even thousands, of years. Careful, alert, I scanned the unfamiliar coast, translating what I read on the chart into what I could actually see. I was passing a shallow bay; further in the distance breakers marked the shoals of Carberry Island, beyond the harbour. Then I picked out a low rocky headland, beyond which the entrance opened up with waves breaking on each side, a line of foam between, and the passage through mid-channel toward the castle.

Just as the way in became clear, the rain that had been chasing us caught up. A squall whipped up the surface of the bay; cold heavy rain hit my face. I dragged on my waterproof jacket, started the engine and pointed Coral into the wind. Then I stepped up onto the cabin roof, dropped the mainsail and secured it untidily to the boom – there was no time for neat stowing. Peering over the sprayhood and squinting against the hard raindrops hitting my eyeballs, I steered Coral into the entrance, past the breakers and through the foam into sheltered water. Just as the pilot book told me, it looked fiercer than it was.

I turned into the wind at a spot clear of the handful of mooring buoys, walked to the bows and let the anchor go. The chain rattled over the windlass until the anchor hit the bottom. As the wind blew Coral quickly astern I gradually paid out twenty metres of chain so it lay along the seabed, and snubbed it around the cleat. Coral continued to move astern; the chain rose out of the water in a shallow catenary, tightened and stopped her. I crouched to grip the chain forward of the bows, feeling the tremors as it straightened out. When it felt solid under my hand I knew that the anchor had turned on the seabed and buried itself (sand and soft mud, according to the pilot book, so it should hold well). The chain tightened further, and then dropped back down as Coral settled into the wind. I looked ashore and picked two features – a rock on the foreshore and directly behind it the chimney of a house – that would serve as a transit line. A gust blew Coral back, opening a gap between chimney and rock, then as the wind dropped back she eased forward again. The anchor had set and was holding well.

As I secured the mainsail properly, coiled ropes, and made Coral tidy for the night, an inshore fishing boat – maybe twenty feet long, laden with lobster pots – came into the harbour and picked up the red buoy behind Coral. There was only one man on board, who hauled the heavy mooring line up onto the bows and dropped the loop around the cleat. I called out to make sure I was not in his way.

"You'll be fine right there," he replied.

The rain clouds had blown over quickly and I took a moment to look around. The harbour appeared roughly circular, sheltered from all directions. On the bay side two low headlands embraced the narrow entrance. To landward the ground rose gradually over farmland and a handful of houses to the low hills of the Mizen Peninsula. A weak evening sun shone through clouds no longer heavy with rain but light and windswept, picking out the flowering gorse against the startling green of the fields and the rough purple of the hills. The ruined castle tower sat on a low mound close to the shore, and next to it a stone-arched bridge under which I glimpsed a further stretch of water. I looked forward to exploring in the morning, but for now I just wanted a quick supper and bed.

• • • • • • •

It was in Dunmanus that I finally got to grips with the shadow of loneliness and homesickness that had haunted me through the trip. I worried that I was taking on more than I would be able to manage, whether it was too early in the year for such an ambitious voyage, and whether I had enough time to do the journey justice. I worried about my wish to find a different kind of conversation with the wild and the world, whether this was an impossible conceit. Would the voyage turn out to be just another sailing cruise? These anxieties did not trouble me when I was sailing, but only at times of relative inactivity, as in St Mawes when we had to wait a day for suitable weather.

I awoke that morning struggling again with gloomy feelings. The early weather forecast told me the day would be sunny and fine with fresh to strong winds from the northwest. I lay in my bunk visualizing the coast from Bantry Bay, across the Kenmare River to Dingle and the Blasket Islands. The wind would be blowing down from Dursey Sound, the next key point on my passage. I had planned to push on again, to get through the Sound today, but I would never get there tacking against a fresh northwesterly. I felt a sudden, stupid annoyance at the weather – it was really frustrating to be held back. Then another, inner voice scolded me, "You read this stuff about infinite games. Why can't you learn to respond to conditions playfully?" I realized that getting to the Blaskets by neap tides had again become the fixed goal in my mind. But the worry took over again, my thoughts leapt forward even further, and I started to plan the journey home. I had been lucky with weather so far, but that might change. Would I be able to get back to Plymouth within the time available now, or would I have to leave Coral in Dingle?

I sat up in my bunk, shocked to find I had imagined myself to the end of the voyage before I was less than half way through! What was going on? Now properly awake, I allowed all the feelings that had been lurking in the back of my mind to come to the foreground.

I missed Elizabeth, her conversation, familiarity, care and concern, her habits and her physical presence. I remembered the everydayness of life at home, like the routine of the morning; getting up early and reading with my first cup of tea, the cat snuggling into my dressing gown; taking a pot and two china mugs to the bedroom, pouring out the tea, putting the milk jug up on the shelf where the cat can't get her head into it; talking through the day together. I missed seeing the tulips coming out in the flowerbed outside the kitchen, the chats with neighbours, the little jobs that need to be done.

I was tired of checking weather and charts. These early morning forecasts thrust the decisions of the day on me when I was scarcely awake. I was tired of making decisions about sailing, each one seeming small but each important: life or death situations might arise from a small but badly wrong choice.

I was tired of this narrow bunk that constrained my sleeping, tired of climbing over the lee cloth to get out, of being constantly alert to the movement of the boat. I was tired of not being able to stand fully upright, of the cramped heads compartment. I was tired of being cold at night, of stepping onto the chilly cabin sole and having to dress quickly to keep warm. And I worried that I might be losing sight of the purpose of the trip: had I got so absorbed in the business of sailing, and in trying to get somewhere too fast, that I had lost the sense of exploring a different connection with the world around me?

· · · · · · ·

I was strangely comforted by confronting my homesickness, by embracing the feelings rather than pushing them away. I climbed out of my bunk and started my morning routine: tea, porridge; tidy cabin, fold and stow bedclothes and dirty underwear; books safely in the bookcase; wash up and put crockery in its racks where it won't fly around, wipe surfaces in the galley area.

By the time I had done all this the morning was unfolding bright but chilly. The sun was bringing just a little warmth. I pumped up the dinghy and motored ashore to explore, finding a tiny cove just by the castle where I landed safely on a pebble beach, pulled up the dinghy and secured the painter to a tree. Leaving my waterproofs, lifejacket and seaboots in the dinghy – it felt immediately warmer on land – I put on walking shoes and looked for a way inland. Scrambling up the rocks I found a footpath, just a track where the grass was trodden down, and a gate onto the road. It looked like someone's private property, so I hoped they wouldn't mind.

I followed the narrow road running along the side of the bay, crossing the bridge I had noticed the previous evening and skirting the edge of the harbour. The castle stood on its mound immediately in front of me, and just a short distance along the road I found the entrance through the fence. An old pallet, roughly hinged to the fencepost with bailer twine, made do for a gate – rather different from the gates on Tresco, I remembered.

The castle seemed to be mainly of dry stone construction, a simple rectangular tower three storeys high, with a taller corner tower attached. High on the walls I could see patches of lime mortar where the walls had been repaired. It had been built around the twelfth century by the O'Mahony clan, who also built Dunlough Castle which I had passed earlier on Three Castle Head. The area had been actively linked with the European economy along the sea routes of the Atlantic Coast since prehistoric times[65], and the castles along the Mizen Peninsula were built near the sea to protect trade and maybe support piracy.

As I walked toward the tower a large black bird flew into a hole on one side; a kestrel hovered nearby. The pointed arch of the doorway looked secure, so I ventured inside. A rough ladder gave access to a higher storey, and I climbed up cautiously, stepping on the outer edges of the treads for safety. There was not much to see but rough stone walls. As I began to climb down an angry, screeching blackness – maybe the same bird I saw fly in – came out of a hole and flew through the doorway into the open air.

I imagined she was nesting, and felt rueful, deeply apologetic. Blundering around in someone else's home, my curiosity had disturbed it. Outside the bird – a chough, with red bill and legs – was sitting on an electricity pole, still calling angrily. I tried speaking to her, saying I had meant no harm, that I would leave her alone now. She stretched out her wings so each flight feather stood out separately, shook herself, and flew back into the castle.

I walked along to the bridge and looked over the water at Coral, with her white hull, faded red hood and dodgers. The Red Ensign was flying astern, the green, white and orange of the Irish courtesy flag fluttered at the cross trees, and the black ball indicating she was at anchor hoisted over the foredeck. I felt a little thrill, seeing her looking so efficient and homely. Beyond Coral the line of surf ran right across the harbour entrance. The other side of the bay was Sheep's Head, the peninsula between Dunmanus and Bantry Bays, a landscape that was becoming so familiar. A thin line of surf breaking on grey rocks marked the water's edge. Green fields, bright with spring grass, sloped up and away from the shore, lined with stone walls and punctuated by the white rectangles of houses and farms. Behind the fields the mountainside rose more steeply, dull brown with a hint of purple here, of ochre there.

Beyond the bridge, the road passed a concrete and stone jetty. Inshore fishing boats were moored alongside, next to piles of nets, lobster pots, the odd faded red buoy, and the assorted necessities of active industry. I had wondered on my way here whether the harbour would be inhabited, reading in the pilot book that this was a 'wild and attractive' place. Certainly attractive, but not wild – this place was home and livelihood to a community of people. It had been so for generations.

A notice pinned to an electricity pole caught my eye. Under the classic red circle with a line through it that universally means 'NO' was printed 'marineharvest'. Underneath in bold capitals, 'KEEP OUT OF DUNMANUS BAY', with the web address www.dunmanusbay.org.

On the jetty a fisherman was sorting his gear, so I walked over and asked him about the notice. He told me that the Dunmanus Bay Marine Association was formed to protect the bay and the wild fisheries from the threat of fish farms. Dunmanus remains the last unspoiled bay in southwest Ireland, unpolluted and clear. "Marine Harvest is a big international company, with farms all over the world," he told me. "They ruin the fishing for others, make big profits, but none of it stays in the area. Big companies like that do no good to local people."

I had come into Dunmanus Bay because it seemed to be wild and unspoiled, a good place to explore my conversation with the more-than-human world. I found it is all those things, but also the site of conflict between development and conservation, a microcosm of a worldwide challenge. The local organization points to the potential destruction of ecology and wildlife, traditional jobs, visual amenity; the international corporation suggests that fish farming will help feed the world, points to the health benefits of seafood, argues that modern methods have dealt with the problems of pollution, and says that local jobs will be created. The locals draw support from many small organizations and are poorly resourced; the corporation claims to be a responsible company, and offers research and professional 'sustainability reports'.

I know both sides of the argument well; we rehearsed them so many times in debates with students on our Masters programme. I am familiar with the good work of people seeking to influence major branded organizations toward greater sustainability – Pepsico, Marks and Spencer, Unilever and others. And I know that the local communities often benefit little from investment from outside: few jobs would be created by fish farms in Dunmanus Bay and most of the profits generated would be exported out of the region.

The arguments between different human interests, between the shareholders of Marine Harvest and the communities of Dunmanus Bay, will rage on. But can we also find a way to hear the voice of Dunmanus Bay and the community of beings that constitute it? If we take Thomas Berry's assertion that the Earth is a community of subjects, Dunmanus Bay must be understood to have a voice. Can we learn to hear it? We might argue that unspoiled places like Dunmanus are rare and thus of particular value in their own right, as havens for threatened species and repositories of complex ecology. They are places where the infinite game of evolutionary development is being played. Can we also entertain the idea that the ecosystem of the bay, as the local expression of a creative cosmos, 'wants' in some sense to retain the complexity that it has created over the millennia, and that it has a right to do so? If that is so, anything that protects the pristine complexity of the bay is good, and anything that harms it is bad.

•••••••

With these ideas running through my mind, I walked back to where I'd left the dinghy. The personal angst of the early morning was now in better perspective, my spirits had lifted, and my thoughts about the next stages of the voyage were clearer. It was Saturday. I would continue to follow my route north toward the Blasket Islands until the middle of the following week, and then make a decision about the timing of the journey home. I might leave Coral on the west coast or I might see if I could make the return journey. Even though the winds were wrong for Dursey Sound, once clear of Dunmanus Bay I should be able to make a northerly course for the big fishing port of Castletownbere. I would make a virtue out of necessity and use the opportunity to buy fresh food and fill up with water and diesel.

Chapter Ten
Dunmanus to Derrynane

Restructuring a system doesn't mean shoving people or things around, bulldozing, rebuilding, hiring and firing – that's not what changes system behaviour. Almost always, the most effective restructuring means putting information into a place where it doesn't now reach, or changing goals, rewards, incentives and disincentives, so that the same people, in the same positions, make decisions in a different way... If you want to really restructure a system – the kind of restructuring that's necessary if we're ever to have a peaceful, just, sustainable world – that means changing the paradigms that are in our heads.
Donella Meadows, *Change is not Doom*[66]

B ack on board, with the engine running and the anchor up and stowed, I steered Coral cautiously through the line of foam across the harbour mouth. Once clear, I shut off the engine, set the sails and adjusted Aries to tack west out of the bay. It was by then late morning, a colourful day, the fields shining bright green and the scattered gorse singing out its gold. Lots of fluffy fair-weather clouds had gathered over the land, and high above them the thin streaks of cirrus suggested a change of weather might be on the way. I knew tacking out of the bay against the northwesterly would be tricky, for the high ground on both sides made the wind fluky, channelling it between the peaks and through the gullies of the hills to the north, and bouncing off the cliff faces to the south.

A port tack – with the wind coming over the port side of the boat – took Coral toward the north shore. Knowing that the hills of Sheep's Head would blanket the wind from the water, I tacked round before getting too close, hoping that one starboard tack would lead down the bay and out to sea. For a while Coral made good progress, gently heeled against the wind. The sails were properly trimmed and balanced. Aries made the best of the conditions, stealing Coral upwind in the stronger puffs, but bearing away quickly as they died away and the lighter breeze backed westerly and keeping the sails pulling well. This is one of the great thrills of sailing, when sails, keel and rudder interact with wind and water so that the boat claws her way to windward.

As Coral neared the entrance to the bay the wind headed her; I had to tack back and forth across the bay, making only slow progress. It took patience. The reward was the elegance of the practice: closing the shore at the end of each leg, neatly tacking round, losing as little way as possible. I was happy while Coral was making good progress and the movement of the boat was pleasurable. But always lurking in the background was the temptation to start the engine and make directly for Sheep's Head. Each litre of diesel contains an enormous 38.6 megajoules of energy that could force the boat against wind and waves rather than work with them. Coral's engine, a solid and efficient marine diesel, served me well, and I never forgot that I couldn't do this trip without it. The question was always there: when is it appropriate to use diesel power, when is it an impatient indulgence, and how do I know the difference?

About half a mile from the mouth of the bay, the wind dropped away and backed suddenly. Aries followed it round, steering Coral almost directly at the cliffs on the southern side. I quickly tacked again, but she didn't pick up speed and we slopped around uncomfortably in the swell rolling in from the sea. With no wind to hold them steady, the sails flapped annoyingly and the boom banged from side to side. The pleasure had gone, the progress had gone – it was time for diesel power. With regret, I started the engine and, my ears now full of diesel roar and the churning of the propeller, we motorsailed toward Sheep's Head.

Once clear of the entrance to the bay, the fresh northwesterly wind reached Coral again, unhindered by the mountains. I turned off the engine and set the sails, taking Coral out to sea until I judged I could turn north and, close-hauled, clear Sheep's Head to make a direct course for the entrance to Berehaven. Coral was working with the natural forces and in the clear fresh wind, and she did so energetically, heeling well over, spray flying away from the bows, harnessing far more power and going much faster than the diesel can ever manage.

I watched as the view up Dunmanus Bay closed behind Sheep's Head and Bantry Bay opened on the other side, for a few moments absorbed in the way the landscape changed shape so quickly. Safely past the head I left Aries in charge and went below to make lunch. Through the lee side cabin window I could see the water streaming past, occasionally running along the side deck. With Coral at this angle it was tricky moving around the cabin to get out the provisions. I couldn't just lay out the bread, butter, cold meat and tomato to make my sandwich, they all slid downhill, had to be wedged in place and put away immediately after use. The juice slopped around in my cup as I poured it, some inevitably spilling. But who cared? We were sailing again, Coral was doing what she does best, and it looked as if we were right on course for the entrance to Berehaven.

· · · · · · ·

I wrote awkwardly in my notebook as Coral bounced over the short waves, my writing close to illegible, trying to remember my changes of mood since waking that morning. I looked up the length of Bantry Bay disappearing off into the distance, at the mountains that rose above its northern shore. I looked back at Sheep's Head with its white lighthouse staring out to sea. "I am here," I told myself, "here all on my own". On reflection I soon realized that the whole point of this trip was that I was *not* alone, that the absence of other people allowed me to be acutely aware of the presence of the more-than-human world. I tried to capture the feeling of the moment, but the only words I could find to scribble down were, "Maybe just being here is enough".

I loved the fragility of that moment, with the wind fresh but not too strong, the waves lively but not huge, the sails and Aries balanced beautifully so Coral held tight into the wind. I loved the sunshine, the sharp blue of the sea, the mountains behind mountains fading misty into the distance. I stood balanced in the cockpit, booted feet wide apart and knees flexed, peering over the sprayhood watching the bows cutting through the water. The wind blew cold on my face but my body was warm in my waterproofs. Every now and then Coral dipped her bows, smacking into the water and sending up sheets of spray that clattered across the deck and thundered into the sprayhood. Sometimes a bucketful would come right into the cockpit; I usually ducked in time, but occasionally got a faceful of water, obscuring my glasses, filling my mouth with salt, dribbling cold down my neck. I felt a wonderful, extraordinary delight that was such a contrast with the moodiness of early morning. I was open to the world and the world poured itself back into me.

At that moment I was no longer talking to myself but engaged in a wider conversation, one that was taking place not so much in words and images as in physical interaction with wind and water. Working Coral out of Dunmanus Bay, tacking carefully to take best advantage of the wind, being open to the conditions and the opportunities that presented themselves, playing the wind when it was fickle and revelling in the fresh breeze – all this was a form of conversation. I was intensely aware of the wind and spray in my face, the thin sun on my body, the response of the boat to the water. Sailing Coral might be seen as a series of questions to the elements: more sail or less? tighter on the wind or bear away a tad? The conversation was embodied in felt forces and physical response; it was an engagement with the world unmediated by language. And it was an engagement that had aesthetic as well as practical qualities – it evoked a sense of beauty and delight, as well as accomplishment.

I thought again about the proposed development in Dunmanus Bay. Large organizations and political systems are incapable of having this kind of conversation. They are necessarily shielded from the direct consequences of their choices. For them, the environment is only perceived through filters, mainly created by the financial systems by which they are judged: return on investment, quarter-on-quarter growth, share price. Of course it makes sense for Marine Harvest to want to build fish farms in Dunmanus Bay if the price is right. And of course it makes sense for the local community to oppose it. They are seeing the world through different value systems and seeking conversations in different languages.

For most of our lives many of us in western societies are separated from the immediacy of our world. We want to go to the shops, see through the window that it's raining and so take the car rather than walk. We drive in the warm and dry, entertained by what's on the radio, oblivious to the damage we are doing to our surroundings – the noise and air pollution, inconvenience to those walking, danger to children – let alone our contribution to climate change. Life on Coral is not immune to this separation: I use the engine and the outboard on the inflatable to make life easier and at times safer. But motoring is always a second choice and is nearly always far less pleasant than sailing.

It is arguable that much of the damage done to ecological systems is caused by what economists call 'externalities': we export the damaging by-products of our activities into other systems and find ways to ignore their impact. The archetypal example is the Victorian sewage system, through which human waste is flushed down the lavatory and transported out of sight to a distant place, maybe simply dumped into a river or out to sea. Pull the plug and the shit disappears. We may think that we have grown beyond these old habits since our water companies now treat our sewage and recycle the water. But we do the same with all kinds of other pollutants. We seem quite happy, for example, to use products made out of plastic, many of which we discard after using only once. Some of them are tiny, like the plastic security rings around the tops of bottles that we tear off and throw away before we can use whatever is in the bottle. As a result, literally millions of tons of plastic are drawn together by ocean currents and float in ocean 'gyres'. Some of it is in large chunks, while some can be mistaken for food by seabirds and fed to their young. But much is in the form of microscopic particles that are ingested by sea creatures – barnacles, lugworms, sand-hopper – thus releasing toxic contaminants into the food chain.

Donella Meadows, a systems thinker who co-authored *The Limits to Growth*,[67] one of the earliest studies to argue that there must be natural limits to human activities, writes that the most significant changes to the world come about by putting information in the right place.[68] In our constructed world, signals of trouble come too late, in the wrong form, and are overlooked or denied. In consequence, the problems build, feeding back and reinforcing themselves, until they are almost uncontrollable.[69] As a culture we took action on fluorocarbons once we had the information about their impact on the ozone layer; we took more notice when we learned that the UV rays allowed through the atmosphere caused skin cancer in humans. We find it far more difficult to absorb the information about climate change, maybe because it remains abstract and not immediate.

The information needed to address such challenges is often expressed in different languages, languages that are incommensurable. Even if we are willing to hear, how can we learn to communicate between the language of business economics, the language of local communities, and the language of endangered ecosystems like Dunmanus Bay?

• • • • • • •

Coral stormed across Bantry Bay and through the western entrance of Berehaven – a channel about five miles long between Bere Island and the mainland – and into the protected waters beyond. Her speed slackened in the lighter winds and she sailed more decorously toward Castletownbere, which is further sheltered behind Dinish Island. I steered Coral through the very narrow entrance, lining up the beacons – two white boards with red stripes on the shore – and followed the safe course they mark past the underwater rocks. Once through, the town clustered around the harbour opened in front of me. To port, lined up along the quay, were some twelve fishing boats, for this is one of the major fishing ports in Northern Europe. Four or five big ocean trawlers, high prows and bulbous bows showing off their seagoing qualities, were moored alongside other smaller, handier inshore vessels. All were smartly painted in bright colours: red, blue, green, maroon.

Castletownbere is a working port and the facilities for yachts are minimal. As is so often the case, the area designated for anchoring was scattered with mooring buoys and it took me quite a while to find a place to anchor safely, between the lifeboat and the ferry slip. Once settled, I took the dinghy ashore to fill my water containers and to find a place to buy diesel. The town was busy – families packed in cars, bars spilling drinkers onto the pavements, young people sitting around eating ice creams – and I realized it was Easter Saturday and a fine warm day for the holiday. Presumably that was also why the fishing boats were all in port.

I felt out of place in this company – grubby and dishevelled, weather-beaten, my hair all over the place and a substantial growth of beard. While everyone else was on holiday, sitting around lazily, I ferried water, diesel, and then food from the supermarket out to Coral. The landing steps were slippery with seaweed. Each time I came to them I stepped cautiously ashore and tied the dinghy painter to one of the large mooring rings on the breakwater. A gaggle of teenage girls were gathered on a park bench at the top of the steps. They were doubtless not in the least interested in this scruffy elderly man, but I nevertheless felt watched and self-conscious as I lugged the full containers down the steps and into the dinghy. I imagined they were waiting for me to slip and anticipated their suppressed laughter as I tumbled in the water. So once I had done my errands I stayed on board and enjoyed the afternoon sunshine on my own. I was later tempted to go ashore for a civilized evening meal – Castletownbere is well known for its restaurants – but preferred to continue in my hermit-like solitude.

• • • • • • •

I awoke to a bright and clear morning. The water in the harbour was completely still, reflecting the colours of the fishing boats and the houses along the shore, but the weather forecast told me that another frontal trough was approaching the west coast. Sure enough, when I came back on deck after breakfast, low cloud and mist had enveloped the harbour.

As I followed the leading lines in reverse out into Castletownbere, a fine rain penetrated everything. Thicker cloud hung around the gullies. I checked there was enough visibility for safety: the entrance to Berehaven, at least a mile ahead of me, was clear, but the further horizon disappeared in the mist. Out in the bay I turned westwards and as I passed Fair Head I could just make out the next headland – Black Ball Head – four or five miles away. Enough visibility to carry on. I was travelling through a landscape of shapes without features. The forms of the headlands and of trees and houses on land were clear enough, but the details were obscured in shades of very green grey.

The weather changed again quickly as the front passed. The outline of Black Ball Head sharpened and a sudden patch of light caught the land. At the same moment I felt the warmth of the sun on my face, my eyes squinting at the brightness. A hint of blue appeared on the horizon behind the head and released the colour in the grass and rocks. A few minutes later the sky to the north and west turned a delicious azure, going down to pale blue. The long streaks of damp grey that clung to the land gave way to fluffy cumulus – white above, still full of rain below – trailing intricate shadows across the fields. Over to the south and west the gloom still came right down to the horizon; south and east the sun was trying to break through thinning cloud. Right behind me, Bere Island remained enveloped in darkness.

I love the way that, out at sea, I can often see the whole of a weather system as it passes. The experience is not just of local effects – now raining, now misty, now sunny – with an accompanying judgment – lovely day, dreadful weather. It's a pattern of change that has form and meaning, once you see the whole. I had watched and been engaged with this low-pressure trough since it covered everything in close mist, and now felt part of its unfolding into bright sky and fair weather clouds. It was an erotic, engaged appreciation, almost a feeling of love – although, as was evident, contrary winds can also infuriate me.

I sat in the cockpit enjoying the arrival of the fine weather, motoring down the coast toward Dursey Sound. I made for a headland with a rock off it in the distance, thinking it was Crow Head, which I had to go around to enter the Sound. But it seemed a long way off. Surely, I thought, I should be there by now?

When I checked my position on the GPS I became confused and disoriented: the waypoint I had entered off Crow Head was to the east of me. It should have been to the west! It took me a little while to realize that, dreaming about the weather, I had motored too far, and was halfway to Dursey Head itself.

Castigating myself for not paying attention, I retraced my course back toward the Sound. Then the alarm buzzed for the mid-day weather forecast. I switched on the radio but heard only Irish fiddle music. After waiting for about five minutes I realized I had set the time an hour wrong. "A gypsy's warning," I told myself, "two mistakes in the space of half an hour". Just because the weather has turned fine there was no excuse for carelessness.

I followed the sailing directions into Dursey Sound, and the intricacies of pilotage focused my attention. It is easy to miss, as the bay that leads to the narrows at first shows no sign of a way through. The Sound itself presented no problems, but the seas at the north entrance were surprisingly turbulent with cross currents and short waves throwing Coral about. Further out into the Kenmare River the water became calmer again: there was no wind, but with good visibility I steered Coral toward the northern shore.

The entrance to Derrynane Harbour leaves Muckiv rocks to port and a reef called Bulligmore to starboard. Muckiv is easy to see because the surf breaks continually. Bulligmore is more dangerous, for it remains out of sight underwater, breaking only in rough weather. The sailing directions advise staying well offshore until you are on the leading line between these hazards and through the narrow entrance. I looked out for the two white markers, brought them into line, and followed them in. I stared hard at the place where Bulligmore should be and saw no rocks, but a treacherous welling up of the sea surface and a swirl of water as I motored past.

Chapter Eleven
Derrynane to Ventry

Heaven is my father and earth is my mother, and even such a small being as I finds an intimate place in their midst. Therefore, that which fills the universe I regard as my body and that which directs the universe I regard as my nature. All people are my brothers and sisters, and all things are my companions.
Chang Tsai, *Western Inscription*[70]

My night at Derrynane was restless – a strong northwest wind blew down the mountains and Coral fetched up hard, jerking on her anchor chain. She rolled and pitched, swung around, getting much closer to an inshore fishing boat on a nearby buoy than I was happy with. Eventually I slept, and awoke later than usual having missed the early morning weather forecast. Rather out of sorts, I climbed out of my bunk and looked outside: not a wonderful day, I thought, with the sky overcast and now a complete calm in the harbour, so no wind to sail. I was on the point of being overtaken by early morning grumpiness again, and I started to laugh – what had come over me? I was in this beautiful place, safe and warm. I didn't have to do anything or go anywhere.

I made porridge, leaving it to sit simmering on the cooker while I drank my cup of tea. After breakfast my mood had improved and so had my estimation of the day. I decided to trust the information from yesterday's forecast that there would be northeasterly winds. A good day, then, to make the next leg around the headlands to Valentia, or beyond into Dingle Bay.

I hauled up the anchor hand over hand, enjoying how it stretched my muscles and got my body moving. Then I carefully followed the leading line out of the harbour, keeping the two white beacons in line astern and passing very close to the reef on the westward side of the entrance. After the winds of the night before, a moderate swell was rolling in, and the sea surged up and down the rocks as Coral passed close by. As she rose on each wave I felt as though I was actually looking down at the water sucking around the rocks, barnacles clinging to their wet surface. Each time the solid water of a wave retreated, I watched the white foam hang in the jagged rocky crevasses, then fall back in tiny glistening waterfalls to join the sea again. In much more of a swell the entrance would be dangerous.

Once well clear of the hazards I turned west toward Bolus Head. Although still no wind, the sky was clearing from the west. I had a moment to look around me at the coast to the north stretching westward from Derrynane to Hogs Head, backed by a row of mountains. Halfway up the slope I noticed a row of houses marking a straight dividing line. Above them rose the rocky, uncultivated land of the mountain, steep, rough, patchy brown. Below, stone walls criss-crossed fields dropping gently to the low cliffs at the edge of the sea. Further along on Hogs Head, sunlight fell more strongly on another cluster of houses nestled in a hollow in the hillside, picking them out bright against dull browny-green fields. The fields themselves were strewn with boulders. This land is beautiful, but it must have been really tough work to make a living from farming it.

As we left the shelter of Hogs Head to cross the entrance to Ballinskelligs Bay the wind arrived, from the northeast as expected and across the beam, filling the sails for a reach toward Bolus Head. I could now see clearly in all directions, back up the Kenmare River, south to Dursey Head, and west to the Skelligs in the far distance. It was a beautiful morning. Coral bubbled along through the water happily, which made me happy too: my early grumpiness and yesterday's homesickness dropped away with the sea and the sailing. For a moment I was tempted to carry on this fast reach right out to the Skelligs, but decided to stick to my plan and continue northwards.

Bolus Head itself loomed ahead on the starboard bow. The pilot book warned me that the cliffs between Derrynane and Dingle Bay are high and spectacular, but I was taken aback, not expecting to see such an enormous bulk of rock towering above me. Bolus is another eroded fold in the geological strata: the rockface on the eastern face, toward the morning sun, rises from the sea in vertical flat planes, as if carefully split; the end of the head facing the ocean is rough hewn where the sea has broken the rock away. Even though I kept a good distance off, we passed into the wind-shadow of the headland and Coral's speed dropped back. Slowly rounding the head, we ventured out into the Atlantic proper and into the ocean swell that rolled around Bolus toward us. It was only a moderate swell, but as each wave approached, higher, it seemed, than Coral's mast, it blocked off the view. Its peak became the visible horizon: I could see nothing but the water in front and the mass of the cliff above. Coral lifted her bows, rose up the slope of the wave, and for a moment we were on top of the world. I could see clearly in all directions. And then we disappeared again, down the back slope of the swell and deeply into the trough, the wider world hidden from us again.

There was nothing dangerous about this swell. The water was not rough, the waves not breaking. But quite suddenly I felt overwhelmed: the headland, the swell, the sky above were all so massive. How tiny we were, little Coral and me, in these rolling waves and this mass of headland. I had been chatting into my audio recorder to make notes about what I could see, but I was silenced by this awesome contrast of size.

And within seconds, I spotted a bird in the water ahead, just a dot at first, then I saw its strange coloured beak and I realized it was my first puffin. I sang out to myself like a five-year-old, "It's a puffin, it's a puffin!"

I had never been in puffin-inhabited seas this early in the year when they come from the ocean to nest. I was overawed and overexcited at the same time and had to calm myself down to attend to my navigation.

'Wilderness treats me like a human being' unfolded in another dimension. The headland and the rolling swell put me firmly in my inconsequential place; the puffin gave me a child-like thrill. With skill and experience, information and the right equipment, I could safely navigate this hugeness, make sense of it, appreciate its loveliness, delight in and feel humbled by it.

· · · · · · ·

At this moment I experienced Bolus Head and the Atlantic swell not as things in the world, but as presences with which I was required to negotiate. The world around me took on a subjective presence. And I thought of Coral and myself as 'we', for now she was not just a machine for navigating the seas, more a companion in my adventures.

The modern worldview, based as it is on materialist assumptions and scientific method, would tell me that this is a romantic conceit. The objects of nature are composed of inert matter, operating according to causal laws. The idea that a cliff, a headland, has presence, in the sense of any meaning for itself, is inconceivable. The notion that Coral is any more than a machine assembled by human ingenuity, useful and effective for my purposes, is anthropomorphism of the most foolish kind.

But Mary Midgley tells us that worldviews are not just abstract philosophical positions; they are guiding myths and imaginative visions. They deeply influence our sense of who we are, our place in the world, what kind of universe we live in and what is ultimately important to us. They are the stories we tell about ourselves and our world which are embedded in everyday assumptions and language. If we consider the material parts of the planet to be brute things, even 'natural resources' – as we do – it is difficult or impossible see that same material either as interacting in a larger ecological system, or as part of a sacred planet.

About ten years ago, I sat on the low wall outside a hotel in the Southern Appalachians waiting for Thomas Berry. Thomas was a Catholic priest and monk in the Passionist order who called himself a geologian or 'Earth scholar'. I count him among my greatest intellectual and spiritual teachers, although I only met him personally this once. He died in 2010 aged 94.

The previous evening I had flown down from New York and Thomas had met me at the airport. I had come to interview him and write an article about his new book, *The Great Work*.[71] In this he emphasized that the task of our time, to which all humans are called in some way, is to restore the balance in human-Earth relations and heal the devastating impact of human activities on planetary ecosystems.

"Let's go and have a beer," he said as he greeted me. This was maybe the last thing I expected of him. I was thinking I had come to meet a Great Man, and here we were going off to a bar! We chatted for a while, and I was completely bowled over by his charm and generosity. He dropped me at my hotel and we arranged to meet next morning for breakfast.

From my seat on the wall in the autumn South Carolina sun, the trees bright with the red and gold of the fall, I watched him drive his rather battered silver Honda into the car park. At the time Thomas was in his mid-eighties. He was not a large man and his emphysema and difficulties with breathing made him seem physically fragile. Nevertheless, he had a strong presence, scholarly, saintly and radical in his views. He walked toward me with a broad smile of greeting over his lined and battered face.

We didn't go in to breakfast straight away. He just came and sat down next to me on the wall and launched into a long explanation of his understanding of the nature of the universe. I panicked, for I did not have my audio recorder with me, but then relaxed and simply listened. I knew the story he was going to tell me, since I had read all his books, studying them again in preparation for this visit. But sitting on the wall together, listening to him explain this to me, was very special. I felt I was being initiated into an understanding that I could never have got from just reading. While he used words to explain what he meant, my experience was almost of a direct transmission of his perspective.

Thomas explained to me that it is a mistake to see the universe as a collection of objects. Rather, mind and matter are two aspects of a single reality. The universe as a whole, with its immense diversity, has both an inner, spiritual or subjective dimension – a being for itself – and an outer, physical dimension. There is a spiritual capacity in carbon just as carbon is implicit in our highest spiritual experience. The inner dimension provides the capacity for self-organization and self-transformation that drives the evolutionary process of the universe. This is expressed in its outer being through the matter and energy of which it is composed. These two dimensions are like two sides of the same coin, different but inseparable.

I had read Thomas' assertion that 'the universe is a communion of subjects, not a collection of objects' many times before. His view was that this must be the starting point for our understanding of all things, and the only place from which we can act if we are to contribute to what he calls the Great Work. But listening to him now, I was touched more deeply with the idea that the universe and the Earth should be understood as sacred communities.

Thomas felt strongly that all understanding begins with story, and that modern Western humans lack an adequate story of who we are, where we came from and what our purpose is. He went on to tell me how the understanding of the universe that arises from recent cosmological discoveries offers a new story of human origination, a story with the potential to give meaning to our lives. This is not the story of a static thing, but of a great evolutionary, self-organizing and self-transforming process of which everything is a part. As Thomas' colleague, the cosmologist Brian Swimme, puts it, 'you take hydrogen gas and you leave it alone and it turns into rosebushes, giraffes and humans.'[72] It is a story in which great transitions occur that are irreversible: the original flaring forth in the 'big bang', the clustering of the first galaxies, the creation of heavy elements in the explosions of the first supernovae, the formation of the sun, the solar system, the Earth itself and the emergence of life. These are all moments of grace through which the universe articulates itself in more and more diverse and complex forms, and from which sentience in plants and animals and eventually human consciousness emerge.

This new story shows us that we humans, with our particular intelligent, emotional and imaginative capacities, reflect one of the deepest dimensions of the universe. It is a story that is both profoundly scientific, drawing on and emphasizing evolutionary cosmology; and at the same time profoundly spiritual, showing how our understanding will be distorted if we only see the world in its external, objective aspect. The universe, Thomas explained, is the only self-referential being: everything else originates in, refers back to and is part of it. The story of the universe is the story of which we are all a part and which every being tells in its own way.

We sat there on that low stone wall, surrounded by the tatter of a commercial hotel, with men and women hurrying in and out as they went about their business. I listened to him straining through his damaged lungs and vocal cords, urgently passing on to me this perspective that was so different from anything I had been brought up with, but which appealed directly to what I knew to be true.

Philosophically, this is a 'panpsychic' perspective, one that embraces the view that all matter has inner 'psychic', 'subjective' or 'experiential' qualities. While the panpsychic perspective contradicts many modernist assumptions about the nature of the world, it actually forms a strong thread through Western philosophy connecting Plato through the Renaissance to the present day.[73] Yet it remains difficult to find appropriate words for this sense of the presence of the world. Words like 'subjective' or 'psychic' or 'spiritual', are contaminated by the dominant materialist perspective when applied to the physical world. One might borrow words from other traditions, and call it Tao, or Atman, or Great Spirit, but this may not offer any clarity and distort the meaning of these words in their original discourses. Or one might follow the philosopher Spinoza – who is often described as the originator of modern panpsychism – and simply call it God, seeing God as synonymous with Nature. But the word God carries with it such strange baggage that is likely to lead to yet another set of misunderstandings. I am inclined to follow my friend Stephan Harding and adopt the ancient term *anima mundi*, literally the 'soul of the world' that permeates the cosmos and animates all matter. *Anima mundi* is not associated with modern meanings of subjectivity, sentience or consciousness, and points to a mysterious and indefinable aliveness permeating everything.

Sailing Coral past Bolus Head I remembered my conversation with Thomas and resisted all those internal voices telling me it was foolishness to see anything other than material objects in these rocks and waves. If, for just a precious moment, the headland and the swell appeared to me as presence, I chose not to dismiss this out of hand. I allowed myself to experience a strange communion with the world, and to feel the immediacy of – indeed, participation with – *anima mundi*.

• • • • • • •

I could not rest in contemplation, for practical matters of sailing safely called my attention. I noticed a streak of white on the surface of water under the headland, evidence maybe of stronger currents. As a precaution, I steered Coral further out to sea where she soon caught the wind as it whipped round the far side of Bolus Head. Now sailing strongly again, I set her on a northerly course past Puffin Island toward Bray Head at the end of Valentia Island.

As we sailed north, the sea became choppier, short waves replacing the regular rhythm of the swell at Bolus Head. The enormous cliffs all along this coast loomed dark and mysterious with the April sun still low behind them, fringed with white surf at their foot. On Puffin Island the seas surged up the cliffs and broke in huge sheets of white that straggled down in ragged waterfalls. At Bray Head and the north side of Valentia Island the cliffs drop sheer into the sea. All along this coastline the twisted patterns and tortured curves of the strata are evidence of geological upheavals long ago.

I was aware of the spectacular cliffs, but most of my attention was with the movement of the boat in the confused seas. In the fresh wind, Coral seemed to bound over the waves one moment and crash through them the next. At times I sat in the corner of the cockpit, holding myself steady with braced legs. At other moments I stood, looking forward over the sprayhood, knees relaxed as in Tai Chi, absorbing the rollercoaster movement as Coral rose and fell with the waves, with the occasional thump as she hit a big one foursquare. Or I went below, clambering over the bridgehead and down the companionway, to wedge myself in the pilot seat behind the chart table. There I could check the GPS, mark off distance and bearing from the waypoint off Bray Head and pencil our position on the chart with time, log reading and course. When I started sailing, these exercises of navigation would be testing points: could I plot a position and get back in the cockpit before being overcome with seasickness from staying below? Now I rarely feel a twinge of nausea.

Somewhere along the coast I made myself lunch. The cooker was hanging on its gimbals at what looked like a crazy angle but was actually horizontal, so I could boil the kettle and make a cup of instant soup – cream of asparagus bought the previous year in Brittany – and tear a hunk off the granary loaf from the bread locker. Without thinking I picked up the rhythm of the boat and climbed back up the companionway into the cockpit without spilling too much – it's a long practiced movement. I settled again into my corner, dipping the bread into the soup. Some inevitably dribbled down the front of my waterproof jacket, but the sea spray would soon wash that off. After draining the last drops, I climbed below again, put the cup safely in the sink and found an apple and some chocolate from the stores in the forecabin.

The wind freshened and it became cold. More substantial amounts of water started coming on board, still spray rather than solid water but sufficient to wash any dirt from the decks and leave them gleaming clean – the sea does such a better job than I can with a brush. As we passed Bray Head and entered the more open waters of Dingle Bay, Aries could no longer cope with the strength of the wind: a reef was needed. I let out the mainsail so that it spilled the wind and Coral continued more sedately under the power of foresail alone. Carefully checking my safety line was attached to the jackstay, taking my cap off – I have lost too many favourite caps to the flick of a rope – and clutching the winch handle, I stepped up onto the side deck, edged around the hood, and half-crawled forward to the mast. Up there on the windward side with Coral well heeled I was high above the sea, so much more exposed than in the cockpit. Another step up to the cabin roof by the mast, I balanced myself for a few moments to tune to the more extreme movement of this forward part of the boat before starting the work of reefing.

Reefing a sail makes it smaller and flatter. These changes make it less powerful and so better adapted to strong winds. Up to a point a larger sail will drive the boat faster, but beyond that the wind overpowers the rig, causing too much heel and unbalanced steering – 'weather helm' – so that the boat turns sharply into the wind no matter how much rudder is applied.

I slackened off the halliard to lower the luff enough to slip the first reefing cringle – an eye in the sail reinforced with a metal grommet – over the hook on the boom. That secured the forward end of the slab. Then I winched in the reefing line that runs down the inside of the boom and through a cringle on the outer edge of the sail – the leach – tightly folding away a slab of canvas along the foot. Finally I took hold of the halliard again and, putting my whole weight onto the handle, winched it up hard. The sail was now smaller and formed a shallower aerofoil that gave less power.

Reefing while under way can be quite tricky. All the time I was at the mast Coral was bouncing up and down underneath me and the sail was thrashing about as it spilled the wind. But I had established a good feel for her rhythm: I wedged my foot against the bottom of the mast, my back against the shrouds, so I could use both hands to coil the tail end of the halliard and reefing lines neatly and stow them securely. Lines are dangerous if left untidy – they can easily wash overboard and trail in the water so they get tangled in the propeller and make the engine useless. Back in the cockpit I hauled in the mainsheet to set the mainsail again. Coral's speed leaped to over six knots again even with reduced sail, but her motion was much more comfortable.

Between Bolus Head and Bray Head I had been absorbed in my body and in the movement of the boat; I had scarcely looked at the magnificent scenery. I realized again how this physical activity – taking care of myself and the boat – was an important part of my conversation with the world. This is so easily overlooked in our culture, dominated as it is by words and sight. I have, over the years of sailing Coral, developed an intuitive sense of when she is harmony with the wind and sea – I feel it in my body before I confirm it by checking the set of the sails and the readings on the instruments. When someone else is at the tiller and is not steering accurately I can have an excruciating sensation of wrongness, and have to be careful not to bark out critically, "You're too close to the wind!" Similarly my movement around the boat becomes increasingly tuned to the roll and pitch as Coral responds to the elements. It is almost clichéd to speak of the rolling gait of a seaman, but I am often quite disoriented when walking on land after being at sea.

Reefing completed, I stood up and looked around me, back to the cliffs of the Valentia headland; up Dingle Bay to the Slieve Mish Mountains; ahead to the cone of Mount Eagle at the western end of the Dingle Peninsula. Peering ahead, I caught my first proper sight of the long undulating shape of Great Blasket Island, the green of its southern slopes dull but just visible through the distant haze. The smaller islands Inishvickillane and Inishnabro further to the west were indistinct in the mist; Tearaght and Inishtooskert were out of sight behind them. For a moment I was thrilled: I had got here, mainly on my own. It had been a fantastic sail today. I was in love with Coral as she continued to bound over the waves. And then doubts set in. "What now?" I wondered. I had planned and looked forward to this voyage for months. Now I had arrived, was there a purpose, other than the travelling? Was this all part of an heroic quest, and if so what was it all about?

• • • • • •

I remembered *The Snow Leopard*, at this moment being shaken around in the bookcase in the cabin, Peter Matthiessen's account of accompanying the field biologist George Schaller, on a Himalayan expedition. The overt purpose of the trip was to study the mating behaviour of *bharal*, blue sheep found high in the mountains near Crystal Monastery where the Buddhist Lama has forbidden hunting. But into the story of this mountain journey Matthiessen wove an inner narrative through accounts of Buddhist teaching and his Zen practice. They were travelling to an area that the rare snow leopard frequents and in part the story revolves around the question, 'Will they see it?'

After a cold, dangerous and exhausting journey the travellers arrived at the monastery and eventually met the Lama, who actually lived as a recluse in a nearby cave. Until a few years previously, he liked to walk around the mountain, but now, crippled by arthritis, he moved only painfully with two crutches. His twisted legs meant he would never again leave the cave. Even so he was cheerful, open, natural and strong, smiling at the Crystal Mountain as he talked. Matthiessen ventured to ask him if he was happy:

"Of course I am happy here! It's wonderful! *Especially* when I have no choice!"

But what about the snow leopard? The Lama's response confronted Matthiessen with a wholehearted acceptance of *what is*, and led him to reflect on his disappointment that he hadn't seen the creature after coming on such a long and arduous journey. Surely the experience of the Mountain, the ice and snow, the sheep and the wolves was quite enough? I recalled the actual words I had underlined in the book:

'Have you seen the snow leopard?

No! Isn't that wonderful?'[74]

As I approached closer to the Blasket Islands I too had to accept what was. There would be no dramatic end to today's wild sail, landing on Great Blasket. The wind dropped and the sea became more turbulent, not alarmingly so, but I imagined how it could be so. The sharp waves kept knocking the way off Coral, there was no satisfying rhythm to her motion even though I climbed up and shook out the reef I'd put in earlier. As the wind dropped it backed northerly, and as Aries followed the wind round, our track no longer took us to Great Blasket but toward or even outside Inishvickillane. For a few moments I imagined rounding Inishvickillane, but I suddenly felt tired. It had been a long, hard day's sail, and there was still quite a way to go before I was safe in harbour. I tacked around and headed up Dingle Bay toward Ventry Harbour, well sheltered and convenient for coming back toward the Blaskets the following day. The wind dropped even more, and I motored the last few miles. By the time I reached the anchorage off Ventry town it was nearly dark. Rain began to spit at me as I dropped the anchor and made everything secure. I went below, closed the hatch over the companionway, pulled off my waterproofs and made a quick hot meal. Looking out later, all I could see were a few dim lights from the village and the loom of the circling hills.

Chapter Twelve
The Blasket Islands

I passed up through the cottages, and walked though a boreen towards the north-west between plots of potatoes and little fields [...] Beyond these I turned up a sharp, green hill, and came out suddenly on the broken edge of a cliff. The effect was wonderful. The Atlantic was right underneath; then I could see the sharp rocks of several uninhabited islands, a mile or two off, the Tearaught further away, and, on my left, the whole northern edge of this island curving away toward the west, with a steep, heathery face, a thousand feet high. The whole sight of wild islands and sea was as clear and cold and brilliant as what one sees in a dream, and alive with the singularly severe glory that is in the character of this place.
J.M.Synge, *Travels in Wicklow, West Kerry, and Connemara*[75]

After settling Coral to anchor off Ventry town I was exhausted. I fell asleep early but was woken by a change of weather in the night. Coral was moving awkwardly, rolling me around in my bunk. A quick look outside told me why: the wind had shifted to the east, blowing little waves across the wide bay.

I found it difficult to get back to sleep – there was so much to think about. I was here at neap tide, as I had promised myself. With the tidal range small and streams weak, it should be easy to explore around the Blasket Islands. But what did I expect? What would make for a feeling of completeness? Matthiessen's story of the snow leopard kept going through my mind: it really didn't matter whether he actually saw her or not. She stood for something elusive, something that could not be pinned down and defined. So did it matter how close I got to the islands themselves? Did I have to make a landing? Or was the elusive sense of their presence, which I experienced yesterday, all I really needed and all I could expect? I reminded myself again that I was playing an infinite game, keeping opportunities open rather than trying to reach a specific goal.

I tossed around with these questions, letting the cold air into my bunk.

Shivering, I pulled a second duvet on top of me. While this warmed me, the two duvets tangled together every time I moved, and bits of me still stuck out into the cold night. In the end I dug out my iPod and played some of Bach's *Brandenburg Concerti* through my headphones. The regular, classical form of the music helped me doze, and eventually to fall asleep again.

The morning forecast told me that once again there was a weak front over the western coast of Ireland, bringing easterly winds, drizzle, and poor visibility. It was indeed a dreary morning. The clouds hung well down, just above the rooftops of the village, and rain periodically rattled on the deck. The sprayhood, thoroughly sodden, began to let water through; large drips fell down the companionway into the cabin. I snuggled under my two duvets until the need for a cup of tea drove me out.

I was certainly not going to try to sail among the rocks and passages of the Blasket Islands in this mist and low cloud. It seemed there was nothing worth doing that day except maybe motoring the few miles to the marina at Dingle, filling up with water and diesel and getting a few stores. I decided to wait until it seemed the rain had stopped, and pottered around with breakfast, tidying the cabin, checking charts and sailing directions until it was time for mid-morning coffee.

At about eleven I looked outside. The cloud was lifting. I climbed into the cockpit and looked toward the west. The peak of Eagle Mountain was sharp against a sudden blue sky. I waited, and over the next half hour the weather cleared further. Soon I could see the mountains across Dingle Bay. Even Mount Brandon on the north side of the Dingle Peninsula, at nearly a thousand metres high, was only covered at the summit. So, with light winds off the mainland, good visibility and weak tidal streams, the day had turned from a grey disappointment into an opportunity. We would after all go to visit the islands. And as the weather changed so did my mood: I felt fit and energetic, no longer tired from the exertions of the previous days, but eager to get underway.

I dressed up for sailing as I did each day. My waterproof trousers might be wearing rather thin, but they felt comfortable and flexible. My leather seaboots were a bit soggy but still dry inside. I didn't need my heavy ocean jacket, but my light, breathable waterproof top, with its warm lining, was still a bit wet on the outside from yesterday. It stuck to me damply as I put my arms into the sleeves, but would soon dry in the wind. Over the top I put my self-inflating lifejacket with its built-in harness. As I fastened the strap around my waist and threaded the crotch straps between my legs, careful to make sure they were not twisted, I noticed a thought, maybe an image, running around in the back of my mind: I might be going to my death.

I could have brushed it aside, but I stopped, sat and waited quietly for a few moments, looking over the bay, allowing this shiver of apprehension to come fully into awareness. What was this about? I was more curious than alarmed, not frightened, but acutely aware of my fragility and vulnerability. The water alongside suddenly looked darker and colder. Every time you set out to sea there is the chance that something will go wrong, or that you will do something silly. I was alone in this remote place, drawing entirely on my own resources. If an emergency were to arise I could not rely on a timely rescue. I felt grateful that I had been given a warning to be careful. It is said that the name 'Blasket' may derive from a Norse word meaning 'a dangerous place'. Maybe a prayer to the spirit of the sea and the islands was appropriate – let me be safe and sensible – and I told myself to hold this sense of foreboding close to me through the day. Carefully I got Coral ready, hauled up and stowed the anchor, and motored out of Ventry Harbour.

The wind was blowing straight down Dingle Bay, so I sailed Coral along the coast on a series of quartering reaches. It took a while for the features of Blasket Sound, between the mainland and Great Blasket, to come clear to me. I could see from the chart that the southern entrance is restricted: a line of islets runs out from Dunmore Head on the mainland to the conical grassy peak called the Lure, beyond which are shallow patches and underwater rocks. I identified the Lure and beyond it a low island surrounded by lots of rocks – that must be Beginish. But the route through was not immediately apparent. As often when approaching a complex passage for the first time, it was difficult to identify unfamiliar landmarks. The chart and sailing directions didn't seem to tally with what was actually in front of me. I should have been used to this after all these years of sailing, learned to be more patient, but I spent several minutes in puzzled confusion, trying to work out which lumps of rock and land were which.

As I sailed further west everything fell into place, like one of those ambiguous pictures that click into clarity. The passage through the Sound opened until I could see Clogher Rock and Sybil Point – the two distant landmarks that define the leading line marked on the chart. There was the Lure, Garraun Point and Beginish. I could see how the passage through ran clear of them all and locate myself with confidence among the hazards of the Sound. I checked the chart again to confirm that, unlike the Lure, Garraun Point, on the southeast corner of Great Blasket, was clean of obstacles.

As Coral sailed into the Sound and toward White Strand Bay at the northeast end of Great Blasket, the landmarks passed more quickly. The two western islands, Inishnabro and Inishvickillane, came into line in the distant haze and then disappeared behind the headland. Shortly after, Inishtooskert emerged to the north. I was still wondering if I might be able to land. There was quite a lot of room between Garraun Point and Beginish, so I took it very gently, standing in toward the shore with the wind on the starboard quarter. The little bay opened in front of me. Above the beach, huddled in a shallow hollow in the hillside, I looked up at the ruins of the village.

The islanders built their homes in the most sheltered spot on the whole island, protected from prevailing winds by the dome of the high ground that rises above, embraced by the low arms of the bay. All I could see of their houses were a dozen, maybe twenty, shells, rough grey stones beginning to tumble down, roofless, gable ends reaching to the sky. They crouched low, bedded into the hillside. Overgrown stone walls outlined ancient abandoned fields. The lines of well-trodden pathways, now grassed over, crossed the hillside. In incongruous contrast to these fading outlines, my eye was caught by three sharply white buildings higher up the hillside with neat slate roofs, bright blue doors and window frames. In the early years of the twentieth century some of the oldest houses had been condemned as unfit for habitation, and new ones built in less sheltered spots. Presumably it was these I was looking at, now maintained for summer visitors. Beyond the village, on the northern side of the hollow, another patchwork of neglected fields stretched from the ridge down to the top of the low cliffs. This land, once intensively farmed, now showed little more than outlines of generations of work and care.

Several books have been written about life here.[76] A small community lived on Great Blasket from at least as early as the seventeenth century, rising to a population of around one hundred and fifty in the mid-nineteenth century. At some points there were even small settlements on some of the outer islands. The community lived by farming, mainly potatoes and oats, by fishing and gathering on the shore, by taking seabirds' eggs and hunting seals. They launched their currachs, built from tarred canvas stretched over a light wooden framework, from a tiny harbour at the end of White Strand. An important additional resource came from shipwrecks, which washed up both valuable cargoes and material from the wrecks themselves.

The last islanders were evacuated by the Irish government in the 1950s, after the community became too small to sustain a livelihood. Even without landing I could sense their presence in the ruins of the village and remains of the fields; and I remembered reading the accounts of island life they left behind. It must have been an extraordinarily tough existence; they were a robust people to survive at all. The fragility of human life in this place reminded me again of my vulnerability. I felt very much on my own, alert and cautious.

I was tempted to try to land on the stretch of yellow sand beneath the village, but there was no shelter. Even though the wind was light it blew directly onto the shore, so the beach was fringed with surf. I knew yachts did anchor here, and there was a landing place somewhere out of the waves, but it looked more suitable for flat-bottomed currachs than for a deep-keel yacht. A little conversation ran through my head – there was no one else to consult – about whether to risk anchoring and going ashore. The cautious part of me prevailed. Reluctantly I motored out of the bay, past low-lying Beginish Island, where I could see another tiny landing place and what looked like more ruins, then carried on north through the Sound.

A maze of stacks and reefs, some drying and some underwater, extend over a mile north and east of the island. Splashes of white came and went as the swell broke over them. There is a deep passage between Beginish and Great Blasket. One of the ships of the Spanish Armada is said to have sailed through safely in the gale that wrecked the fleet, although how much this was luck and how much good judgment is difficult to say. The rocks looked very jagged, and the pilot book offered no directions. An image of Coral stuck on a sharp reef jumped into my mind and I remembered today's prayer to be safe and sensible. If I'd had two competent people on board, one on the helm and one with the chart, it would have been possible, even fun, to find the passage through the short cut, but there was no way I would attempt the intricate pilotage on my own. Instead, I took the longer route outside all the hazards. I skirted Beginish, picked up the leading line through the Sound and followed it until my GPS indicated I was clear of the most northerly rocks. I checked and rechecked my position, scanning the chart for hazards I might have missed. Once I felt safe I turned west toward Inishtooskert and down the northern side of Great Blasket.

Past the protection of the reefs, the Atlantic swell rolled in. The chart here is covered in wavy lines to warn of rough water and overfalls. Alongside is the legend 'heavy breakers in bad weather'. I could well believe it. As each line of swell reached the reef, it softly enveloped the lower rocks, rose up and broke. The wave structure, which had possibly travelled hundreds of miles across the Atlantic, disintegrated into broken water, pounding the rocks with the residual energy of some distant storm. As the water retreated, streams of white ran down the stacks and swirled around the reefs. It was a clear afternoon, with only a slight swell. Goodness knows what it would be like in serious weather.

From the top of each wave I could see all around – to the mountains of the mainland, with Mount Brandon rising above the others, a fringe of cloud clinging to its summit – and at the bottom I could see nothing but sky above the peak of the retreating wave. The only signs of human presence were the tiny white dots of houses on the distant mainland. I felt utterly out of touch with other living humans. I turned away from the mainland and opened myself to the islands. Inishtooskert was to starboard, a long smooth hump with a colossal tumble of rocks falling to the sea at its northern end – I understood why it is called the 'sleeping giant'. The double cone of Tearaght was dead ahead. To port were the huge cliffs along the northern side of Great Blasket, the hump of Inishnabro just appearing again around the far end. Between the islands was a wild, open space, sharp grey waves thrown up by tidal currents. Beyond, the undulating swell of the gunmetal ocean stretched off to the edge of the world. But now I felt no fear or vulnerability, just a simple sense of being here, present in the moment.

I motored down the length of Great Blasket, keeping as close as was safe, looking up at the cliffs and the slopes above. On the southwest side the land slopes gradually down from the ridge that forms the backbone of the island, breaking into the sea in low cliffs. But the northwest side, turned to the open Atlantic, is quite different. It drops precipitously from the ridge in shelving slopes, covered with scant grass and scattered about with stones and rocky outcrops, then plunges to the sea in gigantic steps, the dark rock broken into crags and gullies and set about by sharp reefs.

It was such a short distance between the old village, nestling in its hollow – homely even though deserted – and these unforgiving cliffs. I had a strange and intense feeling of the presence of the past that amplified my sense of aloneness. The people who lived in that village would have known these cliffs and these waters intimately. They collected puffins and their eggs from their burrows on the slopes, and hunted seals in the caves below. Children fell to their deaths from the cliffs, grown men drowned in the caves. And many ships were wrecked on this coast with a huge loss of life, paradoxically bringing a bounty of goods and material to the islanders. All that activity, all their joys and struggles, had vanished away. This absence brought to my mind the transience of human life, and the way we moderns have turned away from wild places except as tourists and maybe as pilgrims.

I reached the sudden end of the cliffs at Canduff Point, the southwestern tip of Great Blasket, where the coastline turns abruptly back on itself. Ahead of me Inishnabro and Inishvickillane rose violently out of the sea, as if the world here was upended when they were created. On the northern point of Inishnabro, pinnacles of broken rock point skywards as the cliff falls down to the sea. They are known, inevitably, as the Cathedral Rocks, because they suggest the spires and buttresses of Gothic cathedrals. But this domesticates them: they are wild far beyond the Gothic imagination.

A flock of guillemots flapped around on their stubby wings. Three gannets flew past in line. I lost sight of them against the sea; they reappeared in the distance, distant white dots against the black rocks of Inishnabro.

There is a landing place on Inishvickillane but I chose not to attempt it. I simply gazed at the changing shapes as I passed, as the broken rocks disappeared and the islands softened into grassy lumps rising from the sea. I sailed on, my mind full of questions again. Did I come all this way just to sail around islands that I couldn't even land on? Should I have tried harder, been bolder? Was I overcautious, or was I wise? Was there any point in coming all this way? What had it taught me about conversations with the wild?

I had a curious response to these islands, although I am hard put to say just what I found so astonishing and overawing. Through the day a quiet feeling had grown in me that they are sacred places. Not 'sacred' in a transcendental sense, with any reference to a god or heaven outside this world; simply that the islands have an integrity of their own beyond the grasp of human comprehension. Gary Snyder suggests the word 'sacred' refers to that which takes us out of our little selves into the wider whole. He also cautions that there is no rush to call things sacred: we must allow the land time to speak to us.[77]

This place had spoken to me through its singular qualities. There was something about the way the land meets the ocean so abruptly; the sense of mystery that held me off from landing; the absence of people yet the presence of their past; the intricate detail of the island passages and the looming vastness of the Atlantic. When I say the islands have a sacred presence I am asking a question. It is a question about myself as well as about the mysterious qualities of wild places, about our human curiosity, about respect and reverence.

In some ways, there was nothing special here, but at the same time everything is always special. I remembered the words John Crook wrote to describe the Maenllwyd, the remote place in Wales where he established his retreat centre:

Peace, quiet joy,
Servants of Silence
Ordinary grey rocks of the mountain
In whom deep waters run
On whom by night the moon
By day the sun.[78]

The islands are quite simply here, on the extreme outer edge of Europe, pushing into the Atlantic. They were inhabited for generations, in that scarcely protected hollow where the ruins of the village remain, home to a community of people who knew how to live here. And yet humans had little impact and very little evidence of human habitation remains. The Blasket Islands are not much use to modern society, and that releases them from being exploited as a resource or utility. It allows for the possibility of re-enchantment. My reluctance to attempt a landing was partly sensible caution, and partly because I quite simply did not feel invited. I even felt landing would be sacrilegious, a dominating refusal to allow them a presence for themselves. It brought to mind resonances of colonial acquisitiveness, conjuring images of British explorers raising the flag and claiming new lands for the Empire.

The islands would be seen as a resource if, for example, an energy company wanted to build wind turbines on them, as was proposed for the Brindled Moor on Lewis.[79] This would open up a conflict similar to that in Dunmanus Bay, where the logic of development runs up against the inchoate and less easily expressed sense of wonder and enchantment. The arguments about the siting of wind farms show that that one person's desolate waste is another's sacred place. I wondered again if somehow the land could speak for itself?

• • • • • • •

I left the islands behind and set a course south across Dingle Bay. My sense of sacredness faded away as I contemplated the several hours' crossing back to Valentia Island. I settled myself into the corner of the cockpit for a long afternoon, now cold, tired, and rather bored. As my mind sank into emptiness I glimpsed a dark shape rise from the water alongside and heard the unmistakable sigh of a dolphin exhaling.

In delight and excitement I leaped to my feet. I saw another, then a group of three. More and more arrived until I could no longer count them. There must have been more than thirty, quite a gathering. Seeking a better view, I left the Autohelm to steer Coral and went forward to stand by the mast, watching from above. I could see the characteristic hourglass line between their dark tops and creamy underneaths as they swam alongside below the water. I watched them surface, the dark crescent of their breathing hole wide open, before they dived again.

There were dolphins all around Coral. Sometimes they followed, sometimes led. Sometimes they rushed from behind, crossed diagonally underneath and emerged alongside the bows in a flurry of water. In groups of two or three they broke surface then dived together, leaving behind a scattering of spray, a pattern of eddies, an elongated circle of wavelets through which they had submerged. For a while a group of eight or more swam in formation, adults and juveniles together, extending in a line from Coral's bow, diving and surfacing almost in unison. A group of puffins was swimming around ahead of us. They caught sight of us racing toward them, and scuttled across the water in alarm, attempting to take off, to get out of the way. I imagined Coral and her dolphin escort as a troop of cavalry, charging across the bay.

What were these dolphins doing, swimming alongside Coral for an hour or more? Were they playing? Sometimes they appeared to be looking at me, so did they know I was there? If so, what did they make of me? I don't think this is human conceit: it is self-evident that in meeting dolphins I was encountering another conscious presence, meeting beings that are subjects similar to ourselves. Even though I could not communicate directly, this experience was palpable – I felt it on my pulse, to borrow from Keats again. I stood by the mast child-like, thrilled, enchanted – literally so, for I was singing out loud to them, thanking them for visiting me, enlightened and awakened by their presence.

We know that dolphins have large brains; that they are intelligent, curious, creative creatures; that they live in communities. We know that they use a language based on sound, and have signature clicks that reveal their individual identity. Yet their world is so different from ours, a water world in which sight is less important than sound, without the manipulations and adaptations of technology. Maybe their consciousness is close to that of early human hunter-gatherers; maybe more mysterious. With the dolphins alongside I knew, felt deeply, that I was encountering a wild, intelligent, sentient presence, another being that nevertheless remained a stranger – for above all we must beware of pretending we can know them. But they did seem to be saying something – about life, grace, beauty – for which I cannot find precise words. Maybe that is the point.[80]

We danced across the water together. Then they were gone, as suddenly as they arrived.

Chapter Thirteen
Skellig Rocks

I know well that heaven and earth and all creation are great, generous and beautiful and good... God's goodness fills all his creatures and all his blessed works full, and endlessly overflows in them [...] God is everything which is good, as I see it, and the goodness which everything has is God.
Julian of Norwich, *Revelations*[81]

After crossing from Dingle Bay with the dolphins, I rounded Bray Head on the western end of Valentia Island in the evening sun and followed the narrow channel that winds between mainland and island to a completely protected anchorage, still and quiet, off the fishing village of Portmagee. Painted houses lined the waterside – yellow ochre, green, blue, deep red, even one a pale lilac – against a backdrop of low rolling hills, the perfection of their reflections scarcely disturbed by tiny ripples. Two or three fishing boats were tied up at the quay; occasional loud metallic crashes reverberated across the water as the crews went about their business. Dogs barked unhappily from a building in the village that appeared to be a small kennels.

A stream ran through the anchorage. In the night I heard the anchor chain grumble and looking outside saw that Coral had swung safely with the tide. There was no wind; the water completely still; a few stars showing through the thin cloud.

• • • • • • •

For the last several days the weather forecast had told of frontal troughs moving in from the Atlantic. When I woke in the morning, the lady at Met Éireann reported a declining anticyclone over Scotland and a slow-moving warm front over the west coast, with winds Force 3 or less through the day. I looked outside. It was bright, with blue sky and no wind at all. The fishing boats had already left the quay, and even the dogs in the kennels were quiet.

The world seemed absolutely still, apart from tiny ripples made by the tide flowing past Coral's hull.

Eight miles southwest of Portmagee, Great and Little Skellig rise over 200 metres directly from the seabed, another relic of the geological upheaval that formed this coast. They have long been a place of pilgrimage, and the nesting places of thousands of seabirds. Some 1,400 years ago monks of the early Irish Church lived high over the Atlantic in stone beehive huts, bound by an ascetic tradition of seclusion that drew on that of the Desert Fathers. Later, a monastery dedicated to St Michael was built there, giving it the alternative name of Skellig Michael.

Should I go to the Skelligs today? I would have to motor all the way, but with the sea calm I would be able to get close to the big rocks. Though I'd done too much motoring, this was an opportunity I didn't want to miss. Portmagee slipped behind as I made my way down the channel and out to sea, which as I expected was utterly smooth. There was not a drop of wind. I looked out to the curve of the horizon, where the sea met a washed-out sky with thin stratus clouds. As usual on a day like this – clear and calm, with no waves or movement close to hand to catch one's attention – the seascape appeared more spacious than ever. I felt not a hint of the foreboding I had experienced the previous day.

I set the Autohelm on a course toward the Skelligs, jutting up darkly from the horizon. Soon local boats, black shapes on the water, appeared behind, roared up and overtook me. They were carrying parties of tourists: I was not the only person who thought it a good day for visiting the Skelligs. With their powerful engines leaving a trail of noise and fumes, the tourist boats ploughed through the water putting up a wash that rocked Coral about. I felt rather silly pottering along behind them. Coral's little engine seemed feeble in comparison to their big diesels. Maybe I should have taken a ride in one of them; I would have been able to land, climb the rocks, see the famous monastery and beehive huts. "I am not a tourist," I told myself. But the line between tourist and inquiring traveller felt very thin.

Once the tourist boats were past, the waves from their wash settled, leaving the sea lightly contoured with Atlantic swell, for this ocean can never be completely still. Ripples were developing on the surface, a slight pattern of disturbance suggesting there might be a little wind. I faced toward it and felt a light breath on my cheekbones. Maybe these were the right conditions to set the big No.1 genoa. It took a few minutes to drag it out from the forecabin, hoist it on the inner forestay, haul in on the sheet and settle the sail into shape so it was pulling well. When I cut the engine –

blissful silence – Coral was trickling along at just under three knots, slowly but elegantly, across a pale silver sea lightly dappled with flashes of sunlight and the shadows of tiny wavelets. And we were going in the right direction too. The tourist boats had roared ahead, but I didn't care: "Let them get on with it," I said to myself, "for we are sailing."

I love this feeling of perfect balance: the mainsail and No.1 just holding their shape, catching every drop of wind and converting the tiny wafts directly into useful energy; underneath, out of sight, the water pressure on Coral's keel resisting sideways movement and the rudder keeping the boat at an ideal angle to the wind. Improbably but delightfully, the hull slipped forward through the water.

The motorboats were using the energy of fossil fuel to power their way through the water. All the energy needed to move Coral forward was coming from the wind, and the only fossil-derived power was the electricity for the instruments and Autohelm. We were doing our best with what the world gave to us at that moment, and I found this immensely satisfying. Surely this is how all our technologies should be, drawing on the energies of the present moment?

We were sailing so well that I could set Aries and turn off the electric Autohelm. There was just enough wind: the vane waved to and fro, its scarcely perceptible movements guiding the tiller and adjusting the course. Now it was only the instruments that required electrical power. A stronger puff and we picked up extra speed, then dropped back again. Coral hung in a delicate self-regulating balance between the elements.

As we approached Little Skellig I could see white dots, and through the binoculars I made out it was almost completely covered with nesting gannets. Other birds were gliding around, hunting fish. Coral slowed right down as she sailed into the wind shadow of the rock. Quite suddenly an extraordinary smell, a combined stink of fish and bird, rotting slightly, wafted over and invaded my senses. Cleaned out by the salty air, my nostrils were hypersensitive; curiously this smell was in equal parts pleasant and disgusting. Closer now to the rock, I saw that the white marks on the rocks were deposits of bird dropping.

In order to navigate around the rocks I had to let go of my smugness at being able to sail, and start the engine again. I passed the tourist boats that had landed their passengers and were drifting around in the water – the boatmen dozing, waiting for the return of their charges – and motored close to Skellig Michael. There is deep water all around, and with no waves and scarcely a hint of swell, I could get close to where the rock rises precipitously from the depths of the sea, sloping at about 45 degrees to twin peaks. Toward the top the slope becomes steeper, columns of rock thrusting vertically upward. A few patches of grass have colonized the saddle between the peaks and the more sheltered places where thin soil has collected.

The rock was dark against the bright morning light, its outline etched against the sky, every foot broken sharply in facets. The sunshine reached weakly through the saddle and onto the rough grass between the peaks, picking out highlights against the deep shadows and drawing out a stronger sense of embodied bulk. I could just make out the path, cut through the rock in an unnatural straight line, and the tiny figures of visitors creeping up from the landing place, incongruous in their bright clothing. Others had already climbed higher and stood in the saddle, outlined against the sky.

My guidebook quotes George Bernard Shaw, who was rowed out to the rocks by five men in a currach in 1910. In a letter to a friend he described what he saw with typical verve:

[The] Skelligs are pinnacled, crocketed, spired, arched, caverned, minaretted; and these gothic extravagances are not curiosities of the island: they are the islands: there is nothing else. [...] I tell you the thing does not belong to any world that you and I have lived and worked in: it is part of our dream world.[82]

There was no question of landing here in a yacht like Coral – even the tourist boats go alongside only for as long as it takes for their passengers to scramble ashore. I slowly circumnavigated the rock, watching the changing shapes as I passed. The western side appeared as if large steps, fit for a giant, had been cut from the peak down to the sea. A lighthouse, no longer used, is perched on one of the steps, a tiny turret of regularity amongst the chaotic rocks. A little further round, the modern lighthouse sits on a lower ledge, brightly white between the dark rocks and the pale blue sky.

Skellig Michael carries an archetypal quality, in the sense that psychologist James Hillman uses the word: it stimulates the imagination. Hillman evokes the Romantic poets' notion of the world as a place of soul-making – a deepening of experience and meaning.[83] Skellig Michael looks as a sacred rock in the middle of the ocean should look: dramatic, isolated, of overwhelming size, full of potential danger. It would fit perfectly into the background of a Renaissance painting or on a Taoist scroll. It didn't disappoint. I felt quietly intimidated.

In many cultures it is traditional to circumambulate sacred places as a holy ritual. For thousands of years Buddhist, Hindu, Jain, and Bön pilgrims have walked around Mount Kailash in the Tibetan Himalayas, traditionally discarding a garment or a lock of hair on the slopes of the mountain as symbol of non-attachment. I remembered how my friend John Crook came back having shaved off his moustache. Muslims walk seven times around the Kaaba as part of the Hajj; they too cut a lock of their hair as part of the ritual. My Jain friends Rupesh and Kajal walked around a sacred fire as part of their wedding ceremony. Of course, I was circumnavigating, not circumambulating, these rocks. But maybe doing this, rather than landing with intrusive curiosity, makes for a form of pilgrimage, of sacred communion?

At the Blasket Islands I had felt completely alone. But now I was very aware of the other visitors. I noticed, with some concern and embarrassment, how I made a distinction between tourism and pilgrimage, that I was smug about my own self-reliance and more than a little scornful of the tourists. It is of course a crude and rather invidious distinction, but I nevertheless found myself wondering about the difference. I decided that as tourists we travel for ourselves, treating the world as an object for our enjoyment. In contrast, travelling as pilgrims we honour the place in its own right, and the place honours us in return. As tourists the point of the journey is to arrive; as pilgrims, the journey itself has its own merit and meaning. On arrival, as tourists we look for entertainment, while as pilgrims we seek wonder and some kind of enlightenment. Environmentalist Satish Kumar calls himself an 'Earth Pilgrim' because, he says, the living Earth in all its grace and beauty is his inspiration and the source of his spirituality.[84]

Tourism, then, tends to be a finite game and pilgrimage an infinite one. Of course, pilgrimage always includes and can turn into tourism. And tourism always contains the seeds of pilgrimage: the sights may be so wonderful as to bend the mind. These rocks certainly have the capacity to shock many who come as tourists into a pilgrimage experience, if only momentarily. They had challenged my capacity for sense-making: Skellig Michael treated me as a human being in the same way as the swell around Bolus Head, by silencing me. I was reminded of the wisdom of the *Tao Te Ching*:

> The way you can go
> isn't the real way.
> The name you can say
> isn't the real name.[85]

I passed outside Washerwoman Rock at the extreme southwestern point of Skellig Michael and turned along the southern side, which, lit by the sun, was altogether less mysterious. I could make out more easily the grey of the rocks, the scattering of yellow lichen, and the spring green grass. A helicopter landing-place has been built precariously on concrete stilts and a walled pathway leads along the cliff face to serve the lighthouse. But high above these I could see clearly the domes of the beehive huts and the straighter walls of the remains of the monastery. I became a tourist and gawped up at these ancient structures, trying to capture them through my telephoto lens.

What do we know about these reclusive monks? Those in the eremitical traditions withdrew from everyday distractions and gave their lives to the contemplation of God. Some argue that the ocean was seen as an abyss, possibly the dwelling place of Satan himself, and therefore that rocks on the edge of the known world, such as the Skelligs, were in the front line of the battle between good and evil.[86] But we also know that the contemplative disciplines of the Desert Fathers took them between inner and outer landscapes in search of a consciousness of the whole of creation. While this is often described in terms of 'living in the presence of God', which can sound strange to modern and non-theist ears, they were also expressing a sense of the limitless beauty and vitality of the natural world and of the deepened, even transcendent, awareness of the self that accompanies this.[87] We also know that early Celtic Christianity stayed much closer to beliefs and understandings of creation from the pagan world than did the mainstream Roman Church.[88] And later Christian mystics such as Julian of Norwich and Meister Eckhart were not dualists: they did not divide the sensual Earth from the heavenly Divine. Julian wrote that our sensuality is grounded in nature, and that through this we find God, while Eckhart asserted that 'every creature is a word of God and a book about God.'[89] I wondered if, in withdrawing from the human culture, the monks on Great Skellig also entered more fully into the wider world, in the manner of the Lama at Crystal Mountain. What a wonderful sense of the divine in wild nature those reclusives must have had, living through year after year in this remoteness.

· · · · · · ·

Little Skellig is rather lower than Skellig Michael, its appearance less dramatic, but the nesting gannets make up for it. There were tens of thousands of them, perched on every level surface – crowding together wherever there was a large flat area, stacked in lines along narrow ledges on the vertical cliffs. They even nested on the top peaks. My bird book told me that gannets space their nests just far enough apart that they cannot reach each other with their beaks. The white and grey pattern of birds and rocks was punctuated by sheer cliffs covered in yellow lichen. In the foreground, birds glided past their nesting partners. I pulled in as close to the rocks as was safe, turned off the engine, and let Coral slop around in the slack swell. As I listened to the sound of the sea and the cry of the birds, I couldn't distinguish individuals, only the noise of the whole colony melding into a continual high-pitched rhythmic screech.

I had not expected this: I'd never seen anything like it in my life. It was the kind of scene one might see on a television nature programme, and I almost expected David Attenborough to appear in the cockpit next to me, urgently explaining the birds' behaviour in a hushed voice. But it was just me and Coral, bobbing around in deep blue water which turned to milky azure around the rocks, opaque where bubbles of air were folded in by breaking waves. Absorbed by the strange noises and pure colours, I watched for nearly half an hour, before pulling myself away.

Chapter Fourteen
Interlude at Derrynane:
What is Wild?

So we can say that New York City and Tokyo are 'natural' but not 'wild'. They do not deviate from the laws of nature, but they are habitats so exclusive in the matter of who and what they give shelter to, as to be truly odd. Wilderness is a place where the wild potential is fully expressed, a diversity of living and nonliving beings flourishing according to their own sorts of order. In ecology we speak of 'wild systems.' When an ecosystem is fully functioning, all the members are present at the assembly. To speak of wildness is to speak of wholeness. Human beings came out of that wholeness.
Gary Snyder, The Etiquette of Freedom[90]

Leaving Little Skellig behind me, I set a course for Bolus Head. The sun, now high in the sky, had sucked up the tiny breeze that carried me out to the rocks. There was no option but to motor across the quiet sea and enjoy the sunshine. That evening, safely at anchor in Derrynane, I sat quietly in the cockpit and watched the day draw to a close. I promised myself I would stay in harbour the next day, and have a rest.

The sun dropped low in the sky. The shadows on the hillside above the harbour lengthened; colour drained away and the lowering light picked out the undulations in the land. Only the ridges remained brightly illuminated; soon they too darkened. In the further distance Cahernageeha Mountain loomed, its southern slopes catching the last gold of the setting sun. The harbour was silent except for a distant dog bark and the harsh screech of an angle grinder from the lifeboat shed. Derrynane Harbour felt secure and homely after the wildness of Great Blasket and the Skellig Rocks.

Those places are wild in the sense that they are isolated, open to extremes of wind and weather; their physical structure is the result of geological forces; their waters are turbulent and potentially dangerous to a small boat. But the coasts of Cork and Kerry have been inhabited for millennia. Even an 'unspoiled' and thinly populated place like Dunmanus Bay has been and remains 'home' to humans, and exists in a tension between development and conservation. Great Blasket may be deserted today, but the ruined buildings and the stories the islanders told remain. And from Blasket I was only a few hours sail from Valentia Island where the first transatlantic telegraph cable came ashore.

Some geologists suggest that the impact of human activities on the planet means the Earth is entering a new epoch that should be called the Anthropocene. Future human or alien geologists will be able to identify a human-influenced stripe in the layers of rock in the same way that the imprint of dinosaurs can be seen in the Jurassic. The human geological footprint will be evident in radioactive material from atom bomb tests, plastic pollution, increased carbon dioxide levels and human-induced mass extinction.[91] Ecology writer Bill McKibben heralded 'the end of nature' – arguing that the stable planet on which human civilization evolved no longer exists.[92] More positively, Thomas Berry suggests that we are emerging into an 'Ecozoic Era' in which humans will necessarily shift from their present devastating impact on the planet toward a benign and participative relationship.[93] Perhaps, as scientist Tim Flannery writes, we will even learn to enhance, rather than reduce, Earth's biological capacity.[94]

The wildness of the sea had offered me encounters with the natural world both scary and exciting. And this is one way in which we humans can approach wild places, as challenges to be overcome. "Why did you climb Everest?" Edmund Hillary was asked after the successful expedition in 1952. "Because it is there," he is supposed to have replied.

Hillary was one in a line of men and women who set out to conquer the wilderness, to test themselves against the worst that nature can summon. One of the most celebrated is Ranulph Fiennes, who describes his exploits in books such as *Living Dangerously* and *Beyond the Limits*. There is a certain unfortunate irony in these titles from the perspective of the ecology, for it is clear that humans are indeed living dangerously and have already gone beyond the limits of the Earth's carrying capacity.[95] It may be glorious and exhilarating to challenge and overcome the natural world, but as a model for our relationship with the planet it is foolhardy.

Ellen MacArthur shows us a rather different path. At the age of 24 the fastest woman and youngest sailor to make a solo non-stop circumnavigation of the globe, she put competitive sailing behind her to engage in environmental campaigning and education. She described in an interview her experience of Georgia Island in the Southern Ocean where she saw abandoned whaling stations: 'It seemed as though we had just taken what we wanted and moved on. That's what we do.' And yet, she admitted, she missed the adventure that comes from being at sea, because there you are so connected to everything around you. 'You are focused on the record, on practicalities, on survival.'[96]

People often ask me if I am scared at sea, especially when I tell them that I often sail on my own, or recount the story of crossing Biscay in a gale. I nearly always reply, "You don't have time to be frightened, there is too much to do." Mostly this is true. Facing the enormous and disinterested presence of the sea, there is no place for a reactive 'fight or flight' response, for anger or fear: one has to embrace the wildness. Once I am 'in the groove,' attuned to the boat, the sea and the weather, I become absorbed in the moment-to-moment practicalities of sailing, particularly when singlehanded. This is true even on those long passages when I sit in the cockpit just watching the sea and feeling the movement of the boat for hours on end. The wildness of the sea opens my physical, embodied and intuitive ways of knowing, so that Coral and I become almost as one body.

Adventuring can be addictive. It can be about conquering nature. But it can also allow us to see aspects of ourselves and our world which are obscured by a civilized perspective. As we encounter the wildness of places – if we are truly open to them – we also encounter our own wildness, which is, as Thomas Berry points out, 'precisely [...] where life and existence and art itself begin'. The effort to tame the world 'would even tame the inner wildness of the human itself.'[97]

The appeal of the wild is, however, relatively recent. Until the mid 1700s cultured Europeans had scarce enthusiasm for wild landscape. Mountains and oceans were seen as dangerous deserts. This relationship toward wilderness changed in the seventeenth and eighteenth centuries as those people who had the time and resources started for the first time to travel for other than purely practical purposes. This trend led the eighteenth-century essayist Edmund Burke to articulate the notion of the sublime, the chaotic intensity of wild nature that inspires a 'heady blend of terror and pleasure.' Nature writer Robert Macfarlane suggests that the notion of the sublime has encouraged our affection for wild landscape.[98]

Most people would agree that the seas off southwest Ireland and places like Mizen Head, the Blasket Islands and the Skelligs are wild, but they would probably have different ideas as to what that really means. The notion of the wild, or of wilderness, has been part of environmental writing from its very early days to the present time, as for example in

Henry David Thoreau, Aldo Leopold, Arne Naess, Jay Griffiths and Robert Macfarlane. In his celebrated essay *Walking*, Thoreau wrote 'in wildness is the preservation of the world'.[99] But wild is a contested notion: it implies a state of nature separate from human interference, and in doing so also reinforces the sense of divide between the human and natural worlds which many environmentalists would see as pernicious.

On the one hand, wildness has been seen as a dangerous force that opposes human projects. Wildness needs to be tamed and controlled in the interest of human enterprise. In his book *Of Wolves and Men*, the field biologist and writer Barry Lopez points out that as the American West was occupied, wilderness became defined as 'the place without God' and that subjugating wild land was seen as 'both clearing trees and clearing pagan minds for Christian ideas'. For Lopez, 'the act of killing wolves became a symbolic act, a way to lash out at the enormous, inchoate obstacle: wilderness'.[100] Yet as Gregory Bateson, one of the originators of systems thinking, pointed out, our attempts to control natural systems will always end in failure: our vision is limited and we are continually surprised when the unintended consequences of our hard-headed choices return to plague us. Because of this we can develop a hatred of the wild, often focussed on a specific creature – like wolves on land (*Who's Afraid of the Big Bad Wolf?*) and sharks at sea (*Jaws*).

An opposing view, espoused in particular by Romantic writers in the nineteenth century, holds that wilderness has special and precious qualities from which the civilized human is alienated, that wild places are full of beauty and abundance. Thoreau writes: 'How near to good is what is wild!' and describes wildness as that which is 'not yet subdued by man'. Yet is it right to separate the human from the wild? While Thoreau praises the wild he also starts his essay by telling us that the human is 'a part and parcel of Nature'.[101]

Certainly wildness can be seen in those places and creatures that are untamed and uncontrolled by human projects; they often form richly interconnected, self-regulating ecosystems. Jay Griffiths writes that she was 'looking for the *will* of the wild. I was looking for how that will expressed itself in elemental vitality, in savage grace.'[102] And, following Gregory Bateson, we can see how human enterprise, in pursuing a singular purpose and drawing on the buried energy of the past, tends to reduce and impoverish those living systems.[103]

The ecological crisis has brought a renewed emphasis on the importance of wild nature. Thomas Berry writes that the human is not here to control but to become part of the Earth community, which has 'ultimately a wild component, a creative spontaneity that is its deepest reality, its most profound mystery.'[104] He suggests that there are times when the human is more confronted by this greater wildness, at moments of transition beyond human control, such as dawn and dusk, at birth and death. The wildness of the universe, he reminds us, is terrifying as well as benign.

For we humans, all these wild places, even though untamed, have been moderated by our understanding of them. Navigating safely means participating with wind and tide and weather, not going against them. The original inhabitants of Great Blasket would have known the currents and the patterns of wind around their island and the capabilities of their currachs with an intimacy inconceivable to an outsider, this knowledge passed down through the generations by imitation and experience. Even the tourist boats with their powerful diesels can only visit the Skelligs when the weather is favourable, for the surge of the swell can make landing impossible and strong winds can actually blow visitors off the rocks.

Like a currach, a small yacht can only work with the conditions. This 'withness' includes the work of generations of marine architects and shipwrights who developed seaworthy yacht design; sailors and yachtsmen who developed the craft of seamanship and recorded their experiences in logs and pilot books; marine scientists and meteorologists who studied the tidal flows and the weather conditions. It was sensible of me, sailing on my own, to arrive at the Blasket Islands at neap tide, and I could consult the almanac to determine exactly when that occurred. My electronic navigation equipment told me exactly where I was, moment to moment, so that even though I could not see the reefs off Blasket Island I knew when I was clear of them. I am part of a community of seagoing people, professional and amateur, who have studied the coast and sea and provided me as skipper with a boat capable of making the passage and the information I need to make the right decisions.

So given the ubiquity and dominance of human presence, maybe nowhere on Earth is truly wild any more. Or maybe we are wrong to see only these special places as wild. For as scientist Tim Flannery points out, all of human culture, including the digital technology of the internet, is part of the long process of evolution.[105] There is no single point in the evolutionary process of the cosmos at which a line can be drawn where a unique human consciousness started and thus between the 'wild' and 'human culture'. Gary Snyder similarly asserts that, 'Wildness is not just the "preservation of the world" it is the world [...] Nature is not a place to visit, it is *home*'.[106]

Rather than wonder if there is no more wildness, maybe we should consider that wildness is everywhere, that it won't go away. When at home I walk up the footpath toward our walled garden, I pass through the pungent smell of badgers and see their diggings at the side of the path. The rectangular ashlar blocks of the garden walls are wildly decorated with yellow and black lichen. The violets growing at the side of the path are self-seeded. Frogs come each spring and lay their spawn in the pond. This wild is deeply integrated with the human: the wild violets are fiercely protected by my wife Elizabeth, and together we dug out the pond the frogs are now happy to use; the stone was quarried locally and the walls built in the eighteenth century. Just as Flannery sees human culture as part of evolution, Snyder sees the human, including language (which is often taken to differentiate the human from the natural world), as part of the wild: 'Language is basically biological [...] Good writing is "wild" language'. From this perspective, the human mind and culture do not impose order on wilderness, but partake in and reflect its essential self-organizing qualities.

One might then say that if everything is wild, if 'wild' no longer differentiates 'civilized' from 'tame', or from 'organized', then it is no longer a useful idea. But while we must refuse to draw a firm line between the human and wild nature, we still know perfectly well what 'wild' means in everyday parlance – it means places that are relatively unaffected by human civilization. Wilderness is a *place*, Gary Snyder tells us, where wild potential is fully expressed. So 'wild' in this sense remains a useful idea because it encourages us out of our comfort zones and can make us look beyond the civilized taken-for-granted. When I took students on 'ecohikes' down the River Dart they reported profound and potentially life-changing experiences. One participant reported: "I thought the core experience was to actually feel myself as part of the natural world. I don't think we normally actually feel that."[107]

The mark of the human interpenetrates with the wild in unexpected ways. William Gilpin, the nineteenth-century cleric closely associated with the idea of the picturesque, saw Tintern Abbey as a feature of an 'artificial kind' that added to the pleasure of the view of the River Wye.[108] My experience is that human additions to a landscape appear to civilize and tame while at the same time emphasizing the dramatic wildness of the place. To my mind the ruined village doesn't prettify Great Blasket, it adds a poignancy to the scene. The stark contrast between the modern lighthouse, and the ancient beehive huts on Great Skellig accentuates the huge strangeness of the rock.

It is not only Western Romantics who saw humans as giving the beauty of the natural world a helping hand. John Blofeld, travelling in China in the 1930s and climbing the stone stairway up the steep rockface to a Taoist monastery, was struck by 'a sense of underlying harmony that was just a shade too pronounced to be altogether natural'. It was all very subtle, though, and he realized that 'Nature could be assisted to achieve masterly effects' so long as the assistance was 'based on intimate knowledge of nature's manifestations'.[109]

In Taoism as in Romanticism, 'nature' is itself part of a human cultural ideal. There is the world of difference between an aesthetic response to the natural world and a human intention that separates itself off from the system on which it depends.

• • • • • • •

The following morning I blew up the dinghy and went ashore, landing on the sandy strip that separates Derrynane Harbour from the bay beyond. I followed the signpost pointing through a gap in the stone wall to a footpath along the northern side of the harbour. The path is well maintained, clearly built to provide visitors with a panoramic view over the harbour. It climbs rapidly between gorse and heather over the rocky outcrop that slopes down to the water's edge. At the highest point, where the path turns inland between two rock faces, I stopped and looked down to where Coral and half a dozen other boats were moored. Beyond the boats I could see how Lamb Island – long, low, covered in scrubby vegetation – protects the harbour from storms; and beyond again, the dark humps of Scarrif and Deenish Islands rose out of a silver sea. To the west a scattering of rocks surround the harbour entrance. Some I could clearly see rising black against the shining water; others were hidden just below the surface, their presence signalled by rising swell occasionally breaking in a swirl of water. On the far horizon I was just able to make out the shapes of the Skelligs.

I took a photo of Coral. By squatting down and framing the picture carefully between the rock faces I could exclude all the other boats, making it appear as if she were riding to anchor on her own in a lonely harbour. It made a nicely composed picture, but I knew it was misleading. For Derrynane is pleasant and homely rather than lonely and wild, a place where the marks of humans – the moored boats, the navigation beacons at the entrance, the scattered houses and fields up the hillside, the accessible footpath – construct a comfortable and inviting landscape. At the far eastern end by the beach, the car park, café and tourist information boards domesticate the land further. It is partly accessibility that makes Derrynane open to domestication: situated just off the main road of the Ring of Kerry, one of the most celebrated tourist routes in the Western world. At Derrynane, the wild has to a large extent been contained.

••••••••

That evening I sat again in the cockpit, watching the day close and thinking about wildness and domestication. I began to see that my voyage had taken place in a liminal space between the civilized and domesticated and the truly wild. This is a space with porous boundaries. The wild can come crashing into the more domesticated, as it does in storms and, even more violently, in earthquakes and tsunamis. The domestic, too, can be taken into the wild, as I had done with my little homely Coral, with her ample stores and comfortable bunks.

Well rested after my quiet day in Derrynane, I checked the charts. Next day I would set off southwards again, making for Crookhaven and Schull and maybe from there cross the Celtic Sea back toward England.

Chapter Fifteen
Downwind to Kinsale

Humans are tuned for relationship. The eyes, the skin, the tongue, ears, and
nostrils – all are gates where our body receives the nourishment of otherness [...]
For the largest part of our species' existence, humans have negotiated relationships
with every aspect of the sensuous surroundings, exchanging possibilities with
every flapping form, with each textured surface and shivering entity [...]
Today we participate almost exclusively with other humans and with our
own human-made technologies. It is a precarious situation, given our age-old
reciprocity with the many-voiced landscape. We still need that which is other than
ourselves and our own creations.
David Abram, *The Spell of the Sensuous*[110]

It was still windy and spitting hard drops of rain when I looked outside on the morning after my sail from Derrynane, and my struggles on the foredeck with the big genoa. With Coral sheltered from the winds behind Rock Island in the long inlet of Crookhaven, I had slept long and soundly. The fresh winds I had fought against to get around Mizen turned out to be a sign of things to come, as I heard from Met Éireann that a deep depression had formed over Spain, squeezing the airflow against the high-pressure that persisted over Scotland. Strong to gale force winds were forecast, east or southeast. There are few facilities in Crookhaven, and I didn't want to be storm-bound there. I pushed against the wind the fifteen miles along the coast to Schull, passing Goat Island and its fond memories of anchoring there with Elizabeth, and through the shelter of Long Island Sound.

Schull is a busy holiday and water sports centre. The harbour is a wide bay with a narrow entrance, usually well sheltered by the many off-lying islands. But the southeasterly blew straight onto the moorings, stirring up an uncomfortable pitch in the water. I was happy to find a visitors' buoy – there were none here when I came before and as the bottom is foul with

161

cables it is not an easy place to anchor. I was cold, and the backlog of tiredness from the long days sailing on my own had been amplified by bashing into the bitter wind all morning. My intention was to rest, replenish stores and to set off for the Scillies as soon as a favourable weather window opened. I was confident, after my west coast adventures, that once I had recovered my energies I could manage this single-handed.

Once settled on the buoy, I blew up the dinghy and set off for the shore. The visitors' moorings are on the far side of the bay from the sheltered landing place behind the pier, and I had an uncomfortable and wet ride. The rough pontoon was already crowded with tenders and large RIBs – rigid inflatables with their bulging tubes and enormous outboards – all jostling each other, jerking up and down on their painters in the lively water. Leaving my waterproofs in the dinghy I walked along the quay to find Simon Nelson behind the counter at Schull Watersports Centre. Simon had the permanent deep tan of one who spends much time on the water. He was quiet at first, as he gave me the form to fill in and took my money for the mooring.

"I'll pay for two nights," I told him, "but I may stay longer. I'm waiting for the weather to cross to the Scillies."

"You may have to wait a long time," he replied, "these southeasterlies are set in for a week or more." We chatted about the unseasonable weather, the lack of rain, the persistent easterly winds.

"Can't remember anything like it," Simon grumbled, "the fishermen hate it."

"If the long range forecast is really bad, I might go home and leave Coral here for a few weeks. Would that be possible?" From the start of my trip I had kept open the possibility that I would leave Coral in Ireland and return to fetch her later in the summer.

Simon was happy for me to stay on the buoy, and told me that the mooring fee would be reduced for a long stay. It was a good deal, much cheaper than I expected. I had been away from home long enough, and I didn't want to wait a week or more for the weather.

"If you do leave your boat here, make sure you use strong mooring lines." I had already seen the pictures on his noticeboard warning visitors not to moor with a single light line, and assured him I had a heavy mooring line with a hard eye at the end that I would shackle to the buoy.

"I'll find an internet café and check the long range forecast and let you know what I will do."

I wandered up into the town, walking along the busy high street with its gaily-painted shop fronts, buying milk, vegetables and a lovely freshly-caught sole from the fish shop. I found Newman's internet café where a friendly woman brought me coffee and a password for my laptop. All the forecasts that I could find online confirmed what Simon had suggested. The pattern of weather was stuck, allowing no possibility of making the Scillies for the next week or more. I decided to leave Coral on the visitors' buoy and fly home.

I spent the next few days arranging flights, a taxi to the airport, and making Coral secure and tidy. My life moved in strange contrast between the calm and civilized internet café and Coral's cold cabin, where I was thrown around as she pitched and rolled in the disturbed water. On the day I left, very early in the morning, the wind was blowing a full gale straight through the harbour entrance, the sea was heaving and I only just managed to get my bags and myself into the dinghy and safely ashore.

I had a companionable ride in an overheated taxi to Cork airport, chatting with the driver about the state of Ireland post-financial collapse and hearing about his passion for breeding and showing horses. At the airport I was sucked into the weird experience of air travel: the forced sociability of the smiling check-in attendant; the passive waiting on a plastic chair with lines of strangers to be told when I could board; and finally committing my safety to the pilots as the plane soared across the Irish Sea. It was all completely familiar and yet utterly strange after weeks of self-reliance and direct contact with the elements.

• • • • • • •

Twelve weeks later, nearly at midsummer, I returned to Schull. After a short cruise around the islands with Elizabeth, I took Coral east to pick up Gwen, who would meet me in Kinsale for the passage home.

The wind was from the west and blustery, blowing in large showery rain clouds – dark and flat below, white and fluffy above – against a bright blue sky. In places an angled shadow underneath the clouds showed where rain was pouring down. It was spring tide again, the streams running fast out of Long Island Bay and between the many small islands between Cape Clear Island and the mainland. With a reef in the mainsail it was an invigorating ride out from Schull, past the Long Island lighthouse, through Calf Island Sound, past Cape Clear Island and on through Gascanane Sound into the open sea. I was thrilled to be out on my own again. The wind and tide, spinning between the islands, threw up short, jagged waves that caught the sunlight and created a sparkling dance around the boat. Passing through the narrows of Gascanane Sound, tidal eddies caught Coral's keel and threw her about like a toy in a bathtub, but we were soon safely through, out in the Celtic Sea and meeting the full force of the westerly. I turned downwind on an easterly course along the south coast.

Sailing downwind in this fresh wind was, as it always is, a little tricky. The following sea lifted the stern round one way then the other with each overtaking wave. Because the forces on the boat were unstable, Aries would not steer accurately enough to keep a course dead downwind. I was concerned that if Coral wandered off course she might gybe or broach to windward out of control. I couldn't steer by hand all day, but I could set Aries to steer on a very broad reach, with the wind coming across the starboard quarter. I could also rig a 'preventer', a line from the end of the boom to the bows, winched tight to hold it steady against the roll of the boat. Our progress was not very elegant, for Coral proceeded downwind in a series of swoops to port then to starboard as Aries overcorrected. After watching for a while I decided she was steady enough to be safe. Everything seemed in order, so now I had time to look around.

We were passing the entrance to Baltimore. I was bidding farewell to the southwest coast, on my way home, wondering if I would ever sail this way again. Astern, a line of cloud extended across the sky, darkly textured grey at each end with heavy rain below. Beyond the lighter middle section I could see clear sky, blue, but greyed out through the cloud. In the wide horizon of the sea I could take in the whole of this cloud system: it looked like the weather would clear after a heavy shower, and if I were lucky, the rain would pass Coral on each side.

Coral's rig would be better balanced if I set the spinnaker boom to goosewing the genoa – pole it out on the opposite side of the mast to the mainsail. I clipped on my safety line and scrambled forward along the side deck. As Coral was rolling rather extravagantly in the following wind, it was not easy to keep my balance. "Am I really safe?" I asked myself, making doubly sure my harness was secured – to the boat at one end and to me at the other. I attached the halliard to the boom, hoisted it and clipped it to the ring on the mast. As soon as I had everything in place the first large drops of cold rain started to fall. Back in the cockpit I winched in the sheet to unfurl the genoa so that it caught the wind clear of the mainsail. It filled with a satisfying clunk. Coral's speed increased by half a knot or more. With a sail set on each side, the forces on the boat were better balanced, Coral rolled less and Aries steered more easily.

Just as I had the sails nicely set the rain began to pour down, flattening the sea but bringing with it fierce gusts of wind. I should have expected there would be squalls under the dark cloud. The log showed Coral's speed increasing to eight, then eight and a half knots, and I watched anxiously – checking sails, course, waves, wind speed – ready to furl the genoa again and take over from Aries should things get out of control. But the squall passed, the sun came out again as promised, and Coral settled down more decorously to her downwind sail.

Along the coast, the usual patchwork of green fields and white farmhouses stood out clearly in the sunlight, but set in a country more rolling than I had grown used to further west. I was sailing some three or four miles off the coast – better to be well clear of the gusts around headlands on a windy day like this. The waves rolled up from behind, deep blue now, their tops blown off by the wind and white foam rolling down their leeward slopes. They lifted Coral's stern as they slipped underneath, then dropped it again as they passed. From time to time a wave broke against the hull, surprising me with a hollow bang.

I felt this wild sea was an ultimate Other, an unfathomable presence I could sense and respond to but whose inner being was a mystery. This is not just so of the sea, but of an animal, a rugged mountain or gentle landscape, the night sky. Unless I encounter wilderness and wildness in the immensity of the high seas, in the leap of a dolphin, in the minuteness of a patch of lichen, I am caught up in a world limited to my own human construction. How then can I have any sense that the world is actually real?[111] For the world may be unknowable, but it is certainly *present*: throughout my adventure it had continually challenged me with that presence, like the squall of wind under the dark cloud.

It struck me how different this direct experience of the wild was from trying to teach ecological issues to management undergraduate students, under fluorescent lights in a windowless lecture room at the University of Bath, where every line was straight, every angle right, the atmosphere remotely controlled. I recalled pointing out the total artificiality of our immediate environment – the environment in which most of their education took place. I suggested that we humans need to be in relationship with the more-than-human, which was not an idea that management students very often hear. If we are no longer engaged – if we no longer hear the call of the sea and the movement of the waters under us – our sensibilities are unnourished. David Abram challenges us that we are only human when we are in contact and conviviality with that which is not human. Without this contact we are in a precarious situation, out of touch and out of balance with the Earth of which we are a part and the creatures that share it with us.[112] Of course, we can sensitize ourselves to the wildness all around us, even in city life. But at this point toward the end of my journey, with the memories of the Blaskets and the Skelligs vivid in my mind, and the wildness of the sea all around me, it was clear that this voyage – my wilderness pilgrimage – had sharpened my sense of engagement to a degree that was impossible in the lecture hall.

The waves kept building, rolling up from behind, and the increasing wind pressed on the sails. I carefully checked that Aries was steering a safe course. An accidental gybe in these conditions would be frightening, dangerous even. All was well, just about; but we were right on the edge of safety. Alert, thrilled, and a little nervous, I felt a heightened sense of the fragility of the space we humans can live in. All around me was the unliveable wildness of the sea. Coral, while she remained intact and properly managed, provided me with a small space of security, even of well-being, between working the elements and being at their mercy. As I'd realized while resting in Derrynane, my whole voyage had taken place between impossible wildness and the security of charts, sailing directions, buoys, lighthouses and electronic navigation. On the scale of the whole planet, all living things exist and thrive in this narrow space we call the biosphere, drawing on the energy of the sun to increase its diversity and habitability. And that too has its vulnerabilities. Wilderness treats me as a human being by taking me to an unmediated experience of this liminality of existence.

Through the afternoon the waves built in size and the wind strength increased. As we passed Galley Head Coral touched nine knots, showing her thoroughbred racing heritage. It was both exciting and nerve-wracking, charging through the water at such a pace. A full racing crew would have pressed on, taking full advantage of the conditions, but I needed to be more cautious and reduce sail. I first rolled in about a quarter of the genoa, and then, harness attached, climbed up to the mast to take a second reef in the main.

At the mast, standing maybe five feet higher than in the cockpit, everything looked and felt more delicately balanced. Coral's unpredictable rolling threatening my foothold; I was not sure how best to hold on. From my higher vantage point I looked down at the bows powering through the sea, turning a wave of solid water to each side, foam and spray blowing off downwind. It seemed that at any moment Coral might bury herself in a larger wave, that water would pour over the decks; but no, she rose to each challenge and kept pressing on safely. Slightly alarmed nevertheless, I tucked another reef in the mainsail to bring it down to about half its full size. With both sails reefed our progress through the waves felt far more secure.

I expected there would be gusty winds and turbulent seas off the Old Head of Kinsale, so I carefully gave it a wide berth. Once safely past I gybed the main – an intentional gybe with the boom under control is safe – bringing Coral onto a port reach across the bay, toward Kinsale and into the river. The entrance was suddenly calm, as was the first mile or so up the river, sheltered by land on each side, but deceptively so. As I motored around the sharp bend below the town, the wind speed indicator shot up to read over thirty knots – the wind I had been riding along the coast now funnelled down the river directly against me. Ahead of me the anchorage was swept into a mass of white, windblown waves.

In this wild water, with moored yachts tossing around and pulling at their mooring lines, there was little safe space to anchor. I let go twice in different places, but the wind blew Coral astern before the anchor caught on the bottom; I could feel the chain dragging along the river bed as she drifted down toward other boats. I had to run back and forth from foredeck to cockpit, getting hot and sweaty, one moment to manage the engine controls and rudder, the next to urgently haul the anchor chain on board, and then back again to steer Coral to safety. After a while I decided to pick up a vacant buoy and hope the owner would not arrive to claim it. Even this was tricky in the strong headwind. Each time I slowed down to approach the buoy Coral's bow blew away downwind, so when I ran up to the bows with the boathook it was out of reach. After several unsuccessful attempts I got hold of the strop of a buoy, and with much struggle managed to get its mooring line on board, haul in against the weight of the boat and the ferocious wind, and belay it to the cleat on the foredeck. Pushed right to the limit of my strength and endurance, I was utterly exhausted, my arms tense and my hands raw with hauling ropes – I was lucky I hadn't hurt myself.

Next morning the wind had dropped and I was able to move away from the buoy and find a place to anchor. I spent the day tidying up and sorting out stores and water for the trip across the Celtic Sea. Gwen was due to arrive the following morning. In the evening, after a proper supper of a piece of steak, local new potatoes and fresh vegetables, I hitched my iPod up to the speakers in the cabin and played Dvořák's *Slavonic Dances* loud.

There is an obsessive quality about a koan. Once you start working with one it grasps the mind and will not let go. That evening I returned to mine to see if I could be clear what I had learned. What does it mean that the wilderness *treats me* as a human being? Without implying any intentionality, when the squall blew more violently under the dark cloud and the cold rain rattled over the deck, I was challenged both in my skill as a sailor and in my ability to stay present and attentive. Open to the immediacy of the moment, the difference between the objective world and my subjective experience disappeared.

The wilderness of the sea treats me as a fragile human being and demands that I respond with awareness, intelligence and skill. It will not tolerate foolishness. This thought brought with it a frisson of superstitious anxiety, as if by suggesting that I am capable of such intelligence and skill I was tempting fate, asking to be tested. It felt safer to say that the sea will always test and challenge foolishness. Only yesterday it tested me when the halliard wrapped itself around the spinnaker boom and got in a terrible tangle. The wilderness of the sea had held up a mirror in which all my responses were reflected moment by moment by moment. It had offered an implacable opportunity for self-confrontation with little respite, little space for carelessness.

And in another sense the sea had tested my capacity as a human being in relation to other humans. Travelling alone had allowed me to be with the wild world away from the distraction of other humans, and to explore my self-sufficiency. I had loved this, felt deeply content and happy and competent in my own skin. However, I had been very lonely, reminding that I am a social being who flourishes in conviviality with other humans as well as with the wild world. At times I had deeply missed the company and comforts of home. I was looking forward to seeing Gwen, and spent quite a bit of time re-organizing the cabin for two, making sure she would have her own comfortable space.

• • • • • •

I poured a large scotch and went outside. The tide had turned and, with the wind now blowing gently with it, Coral lay quietly to her anchor. As I gazed upstream with the wind in my face I heard blackbirds pouring out their liquid song in the trees to my left, and seagulls crying harshly over the river to my right. The stream burbled under Coral's hull, while from across the water came the dull, slow thud of a trawler's diesel engine and the murmuring growl of late traffic in the town. Four men motored upstream in a black RIB, laughing together at a shared joke. The sun shone in my eyes as it sank behind the slate roofs of Kinsale town. Above me an evening sky: clouds, lit from behind, dappled white and grey with just a hint of pink, and the pale blue behind.

Chapter Sixteen
Rough Seas and Night Sky

We are the first generation to learn the comprehensive scientific dimensions of the universe story. We know the observable universe emerged 13.7 billion years ago, and we now live on a planet orbiting the Sun, one of the trillions of stars in one of the billions of galaxies in an unfolding universe that is profoundly creative and interconnected. With our empirical observations expanded by modern science, we are now realizing that our universe is a single immense energy event that began as a tiny speck that has unfolded over time to become galaxies and stars, palms and pelicans, the music of Bach, and each of us alive today. The great discovery of contemporary science is that the universe is not simply a place, but a story – a story in which we are immersed, to which we belong, and out of which we arose.
Brian Swimme and Mary Evelyn Tucker, *The Journey of the Universe*[113]

G wen arrived first thing on Saturday morning. She looked cheerful despite her early start, trundling her case along the quay to meet me. While I had been sailing around the west coast of Ireland she had completed a successful but tiring trip to Malawi, secured new funding for her organization, and established new staff in their posts. She was, I sensed, relieved when I told her that the weather was not right for our crossing yet, and that we would have to wait a while in Kinsale. We spent the day resting and exploring the town, enjoying the narrow streets and brightly painted houses. There were enough people about to create an enjoyable bustle without it feeling overcrowded. We fell quickly into the easy, friendly companionship we developed on the journey out from England nearly three months earlier.

According to the shipping forecast there was a depression coming in from the Atlantic. Fresh to strong southwesterlies would back southeast for a while – not helpful to us – but by Monday were expected to veer southwest and west again, while staying quite fresh. I expected we would be able to start our crossing on Monday morning.

Checking the forecasts and wondering when there would be suitable weather made me anxious. Hanging around – waiting and anticipating, trying to work out when it will be right to sail – is always so different from actively responding to conditions at sea. And there was so much information to make sense of, from Met Éireann, from the British Met Office, from internet sites: at one time the local forecast for the Scillies gave quite different predictions from the shipping forecast for the Fastnet sea area. We also needed to pay attention to the tides, especially as we were approaching springs again. I checked the tidal charts and was relieved to see that they were broadly favourable, flowing east past the Scillies and Land's End during the daylight hours for the next few days. But we needed to get our timing right if possible, so that we could approach the Scillies with the stream with us rather than against us.

On Sunday the winds were still too strong and in the wrong direction, so we went for a long walk down to the coast, eating wild strawberries, warm from the sun, straight from the banks along the roadside. We chatted about our different adventures yet were also happy to walk in silence.

The evening forecast told us to expect fresh southeasterlies on Monday soon veering southwest. Weighing up all the factors we decided to leave around ten, so we would approach the Scillies twenty four hours later in the morning light with a favourable tide. We would have to push close-hauled against the southeasterly winds, maybe motorsailing, for the first few hours. Once the wind had shifted southwest we could expect to make good progress.

Monday morning we hauled up the anchor and motored down the river. Out at sea it was both rougher and windier than I had expected. Coral bashed into big waves, each one knocking the speed off the boat. To make any progress we had to motorsail hard into them. Solid water broke over the bows and ran down the decks, sometimes even pouring into the cockpit. We made slow progress. After two or three hours Gwen started to feel seasick. She kept assuring me that once she had been properly sick she would be better, but became progressively worse and eventually went below to lie down, scarcely able to move in her bunk. I checked with her a little later:

"How are you doing? Do you want to go back, or shall we press on?"

"We've been going for five hours," she said, lifting her head pathetically, "let's not waste that." I was impressed with her lack of self-pity. She really was very unwell, but had at least stopped being sick. The seas had calmed down somewhat and the worst of the rough weather seemed to have passed.

I expected that after a sleep Gwen would feel better. I decided to keep going.

Coral had been sailing close-hauled heading 180° or due south since we left Kinsale; we needed southeast, 145° or so, to make the Scillies. I watched the compass carefully to see what the wind was doing. Gradually, over a couple of hours, our compass heading increased to 185°, 190°, 195°: Aries was following the wind as it gradually veered southerly. If we stayed on this tack we would be taken progressively too far west. After calling down the companionway to warn Gwen so she didn't roll out of her bunk, I tacked Coral round. At first she tracked too far to the east and I watched the compass anxiously, worried that I had tacked prematurely. But the wind continued to veer and settled between southwest and west surprisingly quickly. I was able to gradually ease the sheets until Coral was no longer fighting through the waves, but sailing on a beam reach toward the Scillies.

But Gwen didn't get any better. She told me that although her head was clear, every time she tried to move her body refused to respond. It became evident that this was the beginning of a long night. I had wondered if I would be able to make this crossing single-handed, and in effect that is what I would have to do. Although a bit daunted by the prospect, I was also rather pleased: this was a challenge I could rise to!

In retrospect, I had made a big mistake in coming out of Kinsale into such rough conditions, but now we had to make the best of it. However, after all the fickle high-pressure weather I had experienced on this trip, it was great to have fresh southwesterlies off the Atlantic. Coral was romping along at seven and a half knots in over twenty knots of wind, leaping the waves and clearly loving it.

At times there was a lot to do. I noticed the anchor had come adrift in the big seas and went up to the bows to secure it. As the weather turned a bit misty, I decided to dig out the radar reflector from the forecabin and hoist it to the crosstrees. I went to the mast to take in a reef, and then again to tidy and secure the halliards and reef lines, which had got washed into a tangle by the waves. I was pleased to find I could move easily and confidently – although still carefully – about the deck even in this kind of weather. At other times I just settled myself in the corner of the cockpit out of the wind, taking care to conserve my energy for the long crossing. Sometimes the best thing is to hunker down for hour after hour and let the boat look after herself.

After dark we had a little emergency. Every time I went below to plot our position on the chart I noticed a strange clinking noise. I simply could not work out what it was. Checking around the cabin, nothing seemed to be loose. I was back in the cockpit when Gwen appeared in the companionway and rather feebly attracted my attention.

"I think the noise is coming from under the floorboards. I wonder if there is water there?"

She retired weakly back to her bunk, but was able to hold a torch while I took a look. All the beer bottles stored under the cabin sole were floating in sea water – the last of the Gem ales I had brought all the way from Bath. We had taken so much water on board earlier that the bilge sump was overflowing and water had come up to the floorboards. It took me a good half hour of pumping out, and then scrabbling around on my hands and knees lifting the floorboards, sponging into a bucket and chucking water out through the companionway. "If that doesn't make me sick nothing will," I thought, as I settled down in the cockpit to rest, sweating slightly under my waterproofs. Once the crisis was over, Gwen dropped off to sleep again. I was not tired, and began to really enjoy the crossing.

It was midsummer night. At about half past ten the sky was greeny-grey in the twilight, dappled with clouds. By midnight it was quite dark, and the clouds began to clear. In the small hours, stars appeared on the western horizon over the Atlantic. I wondered if the cold front trailing the depression was coming through and, sure enough, a sharp line between cloud and clear sky moved steadily east. As it passed overhead the wind veered a little more, strengthened, and became gusty. Coral picked up more speed, charging on into the dark. Foam and phosphorescence were glowing all around and trailing in our wake. For a few moments I found it slightly alarming: I stood in the cockpit looking carefully at the sails, sensing the motion through my legs, wondering about taking another reef. The feel of the boat was right, everything was well balanced and the wind was not overpowering the rig. I relaxed: all was well, she was just going very fast.

Once again I had seen the whole of a weather system pass by: cloud and rain gathering and the wind backing southeast as the depression approached; the steady shift of the wind from southeast, to south, to southwest with the arrival of the warm sector; and now the clear skies of polar air behind the cold front. I had experienced the sharp shift in wind direction as each front passed and made the necessary adjustments to course and sails. It is only by staying outdoors for an extended period, in a small boat, or maybe on a mountain, that one gets a chance to experience and be part of this pattern of change. It is familiar and mundane to anyone who understands our weather. But I was certainly not brought up to see and appreciate the patterns of British weather in this way, and I doubt if many people are. In a city it is almost impossible to see the whole sweep of a weather event like this, and in any case, as city dwellers we only need to know if it will be fine or raining. I felt a deep satisfaction in having ridden this system through all its phases.

I watched the stars as they appeared behind the line of cloud, first in the far west and then above me, each one sharp against the dark sky. A satellite moved incongruously amongst the fixed stars. In time, the clouds cleared the moon as it rose in the southeast; I first saw it shining through the genoa, catching full sight of it only when the bows lifted. It was just after full, still large, although waning. A path of pale yellow shimmered across the inky black sea and gleamed on the wet decks. The sky to the east lightened with the moonlight and the stars faded, but overhead they remained bright. I felt very close to them.

I remembered the previous summer's Channel crossing, coming up on deck to find Monica sitting enthralled in the deep, moonless night, as if in a cloud of stars. The wind and rain of the previous few days had left the sky startlingly clear. She told me excitedly about the four planets she had seen near the sun as it set, and later three or four shooting stars. She pointed to another planet shining steady in the southeast, and exclaimed how clearly the Great Bear stood out. I followed her gaze, seeing how the path of the Milky Way struck a line through the sky, rising in the northeast, striding high overhead and coming down to meet the horizon in the southwest. We laughed together in utter delight as we remembered the poet Drew Dellinger's cry, 'I want to write a love letter to the Milky Way!'[114]

That night in the Channel the sky had been completely clear with no moon. But even with a rising moon, while the bright stars of the major constellations took my first attention and wonder, behind and beyond them I could see more and yet more stars. In the end I could make out no black sky between them – a web of faint light filled the night.

After an hour or so the moonlight extinguished all the stars, leaving me musing about what I had seen. Modern cosmological science tells us that as we look up into the stars we are also looking back in time toward the origins of the universe. Incomprehensible billions of years ago, time and space began in the explosion of matter and energy we call the Big Bang. It's impossible to imagine the beginning of everything, but it seems that the universe flared into being and began unfolding into ever-greater diversity and complexity. Galaxies formed, each with billions of stars. The most brilliant of these early stars, after what was a short life in cosmic terms, exploded as colossal supernovae, scattering fragments through their galaxies. Similarly, second- and third-generation stars were born, developed and exploded, and through the birth and destruction of these primal stars the heavier elements required for life were forged from hydrogen and helium: carbon, nitrogen, oxygen, calcium, magnesium and all the others. When one of these primal stars in our galaxy, the Milky Way, exploded, it scattered these elemental remnants far and wide, giving birth to yet another generation of stars. Among these is the one we call the Sun.

Thomas Berry and his cosmologist colleague Brian Swimme emphasise the importance of the universe as story, a story that gives us an understanding of our origins and our place in a wider context.[115] It is a story that draws on the extraordinary, and very recent, unfolding of our cosmological knowledge. We now know that the universe is made up of nearly a hundred billion galaxies, each containing billions of stars. We know that the universe is expanding and that, against all common sense, each of these galaxies, indeed each one of us, is a centre of this expansion. The universe and everything in it belong together in an unfolding creative process, the manifestation of a deep patterning, immanent in the whole and reflected at every level. The universe is not just a space where things happen; it is a process of evolution. It is not based on anything like a predetermined design, for nature itself is creative, exploratory. And here we find new meanings for death, violence and destruction. For it was only out of the destruction of stars that the elements of life could be formed, meaning that at every level the smaller self of the individual dies into and nourishes the larger whole. Destruction and violence are inextricably intertwined with the process of bringing forth more complex forms of order, including life. There is no difference in principle between the self-organizing dynamics of the stars and galaxies and the evolution of life on Earth. They are both part of this creative, evolutionary process, out of which different life forms and then sentience and consciousness emerge.

After the formation of the Sun the story continues. Planets coalesced out of the dust and rock that circulated the early Sun and became ordered into the solar system. It may be that several of these planets were so positioned that life might spark into being, but it seems that it was only on Earth that life evolved as a Gaian process. Life on Earth learned to draw on the vast energy of the sun through photosynthesis, and use it to increase diversity and modify the planet to make it ever more habitable.[116] Because the light from distant stars takes so long to reach my eye, if I could see far enough into space I would look back over the 10 billion years that it took to bring the Earth into existence. It took another 4.6 billion for the Earth to shape itself into its current complexity and beauty.

At that moment, looking up at that fabulous night sky from my tiny boat in the middle of the night and the middle of the sea, I knew that we humans *are* the stuff that stars are made of. This story places humans as emerging from the universe as it evolved. It shifts us away from a purely human-centred perspective and places us back in the context of the cosmos.

I remembered Thomas Berry telling me that all beings have their origins in the evolution of the universe and all bring to it their particular sensitivities. All beings, humans included, are part of a community of subjects. What we bring to this community is our particular capacity for reflexive self-awareness. The human intellectual, emotional and imaginative capacities are part of the universe expressed through the human. We are the universe looking at itself, reflecting on itself, understanding itself, even celebrating itself. But just because we bring this particular gift doesn't make us more important than anything else.

Somewhere in the depths of my memory I found the religious language Saint Thomas Aquinas uses: 'the order of the universe is the ultimate and noblest perfection in things'.[117] Perfection lies both in wholeness and in differentiation; each part belongs to the whole and articulates the whole in its own unique fashion.[118] So humans take their place within the community of beings.

How can we appreciate this story if we cannot see the stars? As Coral charged along through the dark night, I looked up at the gorgeous arc of the universe, back through this ever-retreating web of stars toward its origins and so also to the origins of life on Earth. In the strange starlit darkness of the Celtic Sea I experienced in my heart and guts a deep reality of being part of the whole.

· · · · · · ·

But we had a long way to go, on through the early hours and into the morning. I made one cup of soup, then another, and snacked on apples and chocolate. I found I could take catnaps while sitting in the cockpit, maybe ten minutes at a time. Dawn came, creeping over the sea. Light returned too, but with little colour at first: a dull pewter sea and an overcast sky with hints of blue to come. For a while it was almost day on the eastern horizon yet still night in the west, until slowly the whole sky woke up. This was the longest, slowest, most tedious time of the crossing: I wanted to arrive but knew there were hours of sailing yet to go. I told myself not to be impatient, yet searched the horizon and imagined every dark patch might be land, although each soon dissolved as mirage.

Then suddenly, mid-morning, it was there: a firm presence on the horizon ahead. Quite soon I could recognize Round Island on the northwest corner of the Scillies archipelago; I could make out the hump and just glimpse the vertical line of the lighthouse. I felt a little burst of irrational relief that my navigation was confirmed, that the GPS readings and the pencil marks on the chart reflected the reality of our position, and that we were not sailing forever on an endless sea.

Chapter Seventeen
Returning Home

*... all the regulations of mankind are turned to the end that the intense sensation
of life is lost in continual distraction.*
Friedrich Nietzsche, *Schopenhauer as Educator*[119]

*Have patience with everything unresolved in your heart and to try to love the
questions themselves as if they were locked rooms or books written in a very
foreign language. Don't search for the answers, which could not be given to
you now, because you would not be able to live them. And the point is, to live
everything. Live the questions now. Perhaps then, someday far in the future, you
will gradually, without even noticing it, live your way into the answer.*
Rainer Maria Rilke, *Letters to a Young Poet*[120]

The day following our arrival in the Scillies was bright and windy.
Fresh westerlies whipped white horses across St Mary's Sound,
and the islands stood out sharply against the sea and sky. But the
freshness of colour and clarity of air we had enjoyed in April had disappeared
with the mature vegetation and higher sun of midsummer.

We spent the day quietly, tired after the lively passage, with Gwen
needing to recover from her seasickness. We enjoyed a more leisurely
wander around St Agnes than we had allowed ourselves on our outward
passage, finding places to sit out of the wind and enjoy the sunshine. It
was my birthday, so we bought fresh scones, clotted cream and jam and
celebrated with a little tea party.

But our impetus was now firmly on getting home. Gwen had friends
coming for a weekend house party and wanted to be back in good time
to get everything ready; I was feeling full, overfull, of experiences and
memories, and with the passage from Ireland successfully completed felt
my voyage was essentially over.

As we hauled up the anchor and hoisted the sails early next morning, a man on a nearby yacht put his head out of the hatchway, calling over the water.

"Where are you making for?"

"Falmouth!" we yelled back.

Looking up at the clearing sky and the westerly wind he responded, "You should have a good sail!" and waved as we turned Coral's bows toward the sea.

It was a lovely, bright day with the moderate to fresh westerly wind. Fair weather clouds scurried across the sky making wonderful patterns against the deepening blue. With plenty of power in the sails we made good time. Visibility was much better than on the way out, so for a while we had both the Scillies and Land's End in sight at the same time. Later, we could see right across Mount's Bay as we passed, and as we rounded the Lizard the coast of Cornwall and Devon stretched eastward to the horizon. At the end of a long day we passed the landmarks familiar from our outward passage – the Manacles Buoy, Black Rock, St Anthony's Lighthouse. We took the sails down in Carrick Roads, wound our way through the moorings at Falmouth – so many boats jostling for space – and found a berth in the Visitors' Yacht Haven.

Gwen had decided to catch the train from Falmouth early the following morning, so we went into town for fish and chips as a celebratory final meal. We talked, as one does at the end of any travelling, about where we might go on another voyage, enjoying various imaginary trips but with no sense of commitment. This was a time of endings, not new beginnings. We had enjoyed sailing together, negotiating the cramped intimacy of Coral's cabin where nothing is truly private. Gwen had been a wonderful companion and crew – seasickness notwithstanding – cheerful, willing and uncomplaining. We'd had some great conversations and laughed a lot. So it was a little strange to be saying goodbye, knowing that we would probably not be much in touch unless another sailing opportunity arose. All relationships have their context: we were good sailing buddies, but probably not close friends.

Early next morning we said our fond farewells and Gwen set off to the railway station, her suitcase going clickety-clack over the boards of the pontoon and probably waking up everyone on the other yachts as she passed. I let go the lines securing Coral to the dock, threaded through the moorings and out of the Carrick Roads into the open waters of Falmouth Bay. There was just enough wind for a quiet passage along the coast past Dodman, Fowey, Polperro, and Looe. As we rounded

Rame Head, and I caught my first sight of the lighthouse at the end of the breakwater and the entrance to Plymouth Sound, it felt like a real homecoming for Coral and me. Plymouth received us home gradually. The water at the wide western entrance between the headland and the breakwater was quite turbulent where the ebbing tide met the waves of the Channel. As we crossed from the rugged coast into the softer, more protected parts of the Sound and on into the busyness of the urban port, the water became progressively calmer. At the Hoe, where the city faces the sea, a disused lighthouse stands over the place where Sir Francis Drake finished his game of bowls as the Spanish Armada approached. Here I turned Coral to starboard around the Mountbatten Breakwater, under the high grey walls of the Citadel and into the River Plym and the Cattewater.

Coral's mooring is about a mile up the river at the end of a line of 'trots' where boats are made fast bow and stern between two buoys. I remembered how Gwen and I had secured the lines on that cold wet morning over two months earlier, how the rope had splashed into the water as we let go to start our long trip. Now, I steered Coral carefully alongside and caught hold with the boathook. It was a heavy and messy job to pull the lines on board: they were fouled with a mass of seaweed that had grown on them while I was away. Great bundles of brown, slippery bladderwrack were tangled around the ropes. The weed completely obscured the knots and had rooted deeply into the lay of the ropes. I had to tear it away in great chunks before I could bring the mooring ropes through the fairleads to the cleats fore and aft, to make Coral secure on her mooring. The brown weed messed up the decks, which had been spotlessly clean after months offshore. However much I sluiced buckets of seawater and scrubbed with the brush, flecks of dark brown stuck relentlessly in place.

The voyage was over. All the planning, the hopes and expectations, the excitements, fears and worries had been lived through. During the journey itself I had been offered relatively unsullied encounters with the coast and I was again entangled in everyday life on shore, with its many, often conflicting demands. I now wanted to leave Coral safe and tidy and get home. She had been a companion in my adventures. Leaving everything clean and secure was partly practical, but I also felt I was putting her back to sleep. Safely secured between the buoys, she would wait until the time came to bring her to life again.

• • • • • • •

I live in a Georgian house in Bath, high on the southern hills looking over the city to the fields of Lansdown across the valley. From our windows we see countryside everywhere; even the city buildings are interspersed with trees. On a clear day we can see the Black Mountains and the Sugar Loaf over to the west, beyond Bristol and the Severn Valley. But this lovely landscape is far from wild. Elizabeth likes to call it the "soft underbelly of England". It is thoroughly a creation of human ingenuity and endeavour, fenced and tamed, criss-crossed with roads, railways, canals and powerlines. We humans think we own it, that it is ours.

Sometimes the wild invades. I often watch as dark clouds gather over the Welsh mountains and the line of a weather front moves relentlessly up the valley, enveloping the hills. Sometimes, from the dark streaks angled below the distant cloud, I can tell that a torrent of rain will soon descend on us. Or, walking along the lane to the garden, I hear a distant, high mewing and, after searching the sky, see one, maybe two, buzzards circling way above my head. Toward autumn we are invaded by spiders, who construct their webs between the glazing bars of the window and the fuschias in the window box, and weave intricate patterns between the iron railings at the gate.

One morning in late July, several weeks after returning home, I woke and rose early with the question, "How has my voyage changed me?" pulsing through my mind. I went downstairs in the morning quiet. Even the cat was not awake yet. I put on the kettle for tea, unlocked the back door and stepped outside in my dressing gown into the pleasant coolness, looking over Bath and along the valley toward Bristol. The day was dry and bright; a regular pattern of small cumulus covered the sky. The nicotiana in the flowerbed were just coming out, their flowers a creamy off-white with a hint of pale green, their delicate scent rising in the morning air. From over the hedge a blackbird sang. The view was clear right to the Black Mountains. Just a hint of traffic noise rose from the town below, while behind me in the kitchen the kettle roared as it approached the boil.

I made my tea, sat down with Gary Snyder's book *The Practice of the Wild* and reminded myself of what he wrote about returning home: the best purpose of wilderness experiences is seeing home with new eyes, 'as part of the same territory – never totally ruined, never completely unnatural'.[121] Just as I'd seen in Derrynane and sailing back along the southern Ireland coast, we dwell between the wild world and the adapted, cultured world.

So how had the voyage changed me? Was I retaining a conversation with the world or was I losing it to an entanglement in everyday human life? Certainly, the intense experience of the wild world was no longer with me:

I was less aware of the patterns of life. When someone asked me, "What is the weather doing?" I realized I had no comprehensive answer beyond, "Oh, I think it's going to be dry today." I no longer had an intimate knowledge of weather systems: at sea I had listened to the forecasts every day, checked them against the clouds in the sky and the shifting winds, and had a pretty good idea of what to expect. I also realized I had lost touch with the phases of the moon, and so of the tides. I didn't need to know these things to live my everyday urban life, but not knowing them left me feeling vaguely impoverished.

For a while, though, I retained a heightened sense of beauty. The pattern of clouds in a gap between the trees would grab my attention and make me pause to notice their changing shapes, how white shaded into greys against blues. When Elizabeth arranged flowers from the garden on our dining table, I was for a moment captured by the shape of a rose petal, how concave turned elegantly to convex, how the red near the stem shaded lighter toward the outside edge. A few days later the rose had opened more fully. I came down one morning to find the petals had dropped onto the oak table, making a different pattern of loveliness.

At the same time national and international news events competed for my attention. The global financial crisis widened and deepened, demonstrating the insubstantial foundations of our consumerism. For a while the *News of the World* phone-tapping scandal completely absorbed media attention in the UK, presenting a drama on the public stage as well-known figures were swept up by events and resigned. An unfolding famine in the Horn of Africa was headlined, but was again displaced by the news of the rebel advance into Tripoli. All this faded and a murder story captivated us all with ambivalent horror. I felt that as an informed citizen I should know about these public events taking place in our world. Yet they drown out the call of the wild world in which all of us are located. As Friedrich Nietzsche points out, the everyday world and its distractions piles in until we lose touch with the 'intense sensation of living.'

But it was not only at a public level that human concerns drove out my attention to the wild context. Toward the end of July my dear friend John Crook died suddenly, not long after his eightieth birthday celebrations. I was deeply upset by his passing, and for a while unable to accept that he had gone. It was only in January that I had stayed at his house for my retreat, telling him about my encounter with the sparrowhawk and experiences in meditation. He had at that time been still so very full of life. And I know that as a Buddhist teacher he would want us to use his passing as a lesson in impermanence and non-attachment. As he wrote in Coral's poetry book:

Nothing matters
And everything must go
Yet, love is having the heart touched
In the valleys of suffering.[122]

Our human concerns rightly and inevitably engage our attention, but they don't have to monopolize it completely. Wilderness experiences are important, maybe essential ways of opening our attention to our wider context. As I realized on the long night passages across the Celtic sea, the wild world takes us away from our everyday human preoccupations. I was disoriented from my taken-for-granted world by the continual movement of a small boat, the dark, the aching fatigue, the feeling of charging through a blackness with no features that went on forever. Social constructions of reality fell away, allowing a more naked sense of what it is to be a human being.

At such moments it is as if a crack in the cosmic egg opens and for a tiny moment I experience a different world that is nevertheless the same world. It is a world that is not fixed in form, but forever changing: no longer divided into separate things, but one dancing whole. These tiny moments are so easy to overlook, to see as insignificant. They are not overwhelming transformations of consciousness. But they are profoundly important in calling forth a different conversation with the world.

It certainly didn't help to reach for these moments with the rational mind and will. When I attempted consciously to address the questions I took with me, or to 'solve' my koan, I was spectacularly unsuccessful. The poet Rainer Maria Rilke tells us to 'have patience with everything unresolved in your heart and to try to love the questions themselves.' But throughout the long journey, and through holding my questions lightly, I did place myself in situations and a state of mind in which some little understanding might emerge.

I think the kind of wilderness journey or deep ecology pilgrimage I have undertaken is one response to the dramatic and frightening changes that are taking place on the planet. It is not, of course, a sufficient or adequate response: we also urgently need a whole range of political, financial, technological and cultural responses that would change society as we know it. Such changes are within our grasp if we can collectively summon up the courage, imagination and will power.

We will not rise to the challenges of our times until we hear the pain of the world: we need to fall in love again, to re-establish and reinvent our conversation. The shift in worldview that arises from wilderness experience may not be a sufficient response, but I think it is nevertheless a necessary response. Opening oneself to the wild world and describing what one finds with love and passion is, in this view, a political and spiritual act. And we are also giving something back: as Rainer Maria Rilke again tells us, 'The more looked-at world wants to be nourished by love.'[123]

· · · · · · ·

Mid-December. After a mild November when we wondered if winter would ever come, a series of deep depressions brought storms in from the Atlantic. I left my writing and walked up to the garden between the heavy showers seeking fresh air. Despite the wind that howled around the house last night, leaves still clung to the oak tree that Ben had planted outside the garden gate. He was then about eight, and had picked up a sprouting acorn when we were out on family walk in a wood. It thrived in a little plastic pot until it was large enough to plant outside.

That was nearly thirty years ago, and the tree had grown to a substantial size, its branches hanging over our garden wall. The fresh green leaves of spring had crumpled and seemed to glow golden-brown in the low sun, which even in the dead of winter keeps on powering life on Earth. The wind was bitterly cold but in precious sheltered places where the sun catches, I was grateful for the warmth.

Thank you.

The first version of *Spindrift* formed the Manuscript submitted for the MA in Creative Writing at Bath Spa University. I am grateful to the faculty and all my fellow students for making this course such an inspirational experience. I particularly want to thank Mimi Thebo for having the courage to put a line through the first four pages I submitted to her, challenging me to leave my academic style of writing behind and learn to tell stories; Tessa Hadley for creating a wonderfully stimulating prose seminar in the second term; Richard Kerridge for fierce arguments about literature and the crisis of ecology; and most of all Paul Evans, my manuscript tutor, who always had faith in my writing, and firmly but gently insisted that the book be written from the perspective of Coral's cockpit. Paul very kindly wrote the Foreword that nicely introduces the themes of the book.

Emerging from the intensive year of the MA, several graduates continued to meet as an on-going writing group, to provide each other with support and challenge. Each member bringing different skills and perspectives to the writing process. Many thanks to my good friends Emma, Hadiza, Jane, Sophie, Susan, Tanya, Victoria and Vanessa.

Gwen Vaughan joined me as crew on Coral for the two long legs of the voyage across the Celtic Sea. She kept watch during the long April night of the outward crossing, did more than her fair share of the cooking, and stayed cheerful even when horribly seasick on the return journey. We had many stimulating conversations about the quality of the seascape and the nature of the sailing experience.

I am grateful to those involved in bringing the manuscript to its final form. Jessica Woollard of the Marsh Agency, Sarah Bird and Melanie Newman of Vala, all offered incisive editorial comments. The book is shorter and tighter as a result of their suggestions. Rowan Evans did a wonderful job as copyeditor, not only correcting my grammar and punctuation but also pointing out where my writing was unclear and repetitious. Alan Blakemore, Denis Kennedy and Kay Russell provided meticulous proof reading. Sue Gent designed the book as a whole, designed the lovely cover, and drew the clear charts of *Coral*'s voyage. Jean Boulton and Rosemary Nixon brought their enthusiasm, business and publishing experience to support the marketing. Thank you all. Whatever errors and infelicities remain are entirely my responsibility.

Thanks to everyone at Vala Publications. To Sarah Bird for having the idea of starting a publishing cooperative and the continuing courage to take it forward. To our Chair Andrew Radford for leading the Management Board with persistence and good humour from the start, and for bringing an ethical business experience to our debates. To everyone on the Management and Editorial Boards, thanks for time, commitment and creative contributions. Vala is, among other things, an 'experiment in community supported publishing' and all those involved in management, editorial and author roles know they are well supported by the enthusiasm and practical help of the members.

At the end of a long list but ever-present, my gratitude beyond all words goes to Elizabeth, my wife and best beloved, for fifty years of love, challenge, companionship and learning.

References

Chapter One

1. Berry, Thomas, and Thomas Clarke. *Befriending the Earth: A Theology of Reconciliation between Humans and the Earth*. Mystic, Connecticut: Twenty-Third Publication, 1991, p. 20.
2. Marshall, Judi, Gill Coleman, and Peter Reason. *Leadership for Sustainability: An Action Research Approach*. Sheffield: Greenleaf, 2011.
3. Reason, Peter, Gill Coleman, David Ballard, Michelle Williams, Margaret Gearty, Carole Bond, Chris Seeley, and Esther Maughan McLachlan. *Insider Voices: Human Dimensions of Low Carbon Technology*. Bath: Centre for Action Research in Professional Practice, University of Bath. (Available at http://people.bath.ac.uk/mnspwr), 2009.
4. Bateson, Gregory. *Mind and Nature: A Necessary Unity*. New York: E. P. Dutton, 1979.
5. Snyder, Gary. *The Practice of the Wild*. New York: North Point Press, 1990, p. 94.
6. Snyder, Gary. *The Practice of the Wild*, p. 5.
7. Midgley, Mary. *The Solitary Self: Darwin and the Selfish Gene*. Durham: Acumen Press, 2010.
8. Berry, Thomas. *The Great Work: Our Way into the Future*. New York: Bell Tower, 1999, p. 72.
9. Berry, Thomas. *Evening Thoughts*. San Francisco: Sierra Club Books, 2006, p. 17.
10. The environmental activist and writer Bill McKibben argues that the changes are already so profound that we are living on an essentially different planet from the one in which humans evolved and civilizations developed. McKibben, Bill. *Eaarth: Making Life on a Tough New Planet*. New York: Henry Holt, 2010.
11. This 'Medea' hypothesis, named after the terrifying figure from Greek mythology, is explored by Tim Flannery in *Here on Earth: A new beginning*. London: Allen Lane, 2011.
12. There is an important campaign to have the United Nations declare ecocide the fifth crime against peace, alongside genocide, crimes against humanity, war crimes, and the crime of aggression. See http://www.thisisecocide.com/
13. McDonough, William, and Michael Braungart. *Cradle to Cradle: Remaking the Way We Make Things*. New York: Northpoint Press, 2002.
14. The term 'more-than-human world' was introduced by the ecological philosopher David Abram in an attempt to broaden our sense that we are part of a wider world of which humans are a part. Abram, David. *The Spell of the Sensuous: Perception and Language in a More Than Human World*. New York: Pantheon, 1996.
15. I have borrowed this phrase from my friend Stephan Harding. It chimes with Joanna Macy's insistence that we always start ecological work in gratitude, and with Matthew Fox's emphasis on the joy of creation. Macy, Joanna, and Molly Young Brown. *Coming Back to Life: Practices to Reconnect Our Lives, Our World*. Gabriola Island: New Society Publishers, 1998. Fox, Matthew. *Original Blessing: A Primer in Creation Spirituality*. Santa Fe, NM: Bear & Company, Inc., 1983.

Chapter Two

16. Steinbeck, John. *The Log from the Sea of Cortez*. London: Heinmann, 1958, p. 73.
17. Keen, Norman, ed. *Sailing Directions for the South and West Coasts of Ireland*. Irish Norman Cruising Club Publications. 12th edition 2008 (A Thirteenth edition was published in 2013).
18. Harman, Willis. *Global Mind Change: The Promise of the Last Years of the Twentieth Century*. Indianapolis: Knowledge Systems, 1988, pp. 9-10.
19. Orr, David W. *Earth in Mind*. Washington, DC: Island Press, 1994, p. 2.

Chapter Three

20. Snyder, Gary. *The Gary Snyder Reader: Prose, Poetry, and Translations*. New York: Counterpoint, 1999, p. 209.

21. Lubbock, B. *The Log of "the Cutty Sark"*. Glasgow: Brown, Son & Ferguson, 1960.

22. Ransome, Arthur. *Swallows and Amazons*. London: Jonathan Cape, 1930.

23. Bly, Robert, ed. *Iron John: A Book About Men*. Reading, Mass: Addison Wesley, 1990.

24. Keen, Sam. *Fire in the Belly - on Being a Man*. London: Judy Piatkus Limited, 1992.

Chapter Four

25. Meeker, Joseph W. *The Comedy of Survival: Literary Ecology and a Play Ethic*. Tucson: University of Arizona Press, 1997, p. 20.

26. Joseph Heller. *Catch 22*. New York: Simon and Schuster, 1961.

27. For a straightforward account of changes in the jet stream see Woolings, Tim. *Winds of Change?* Planet Earth, Winter 2010, pp. 18-19. Available at http://www.met.reading.ac.uk/~swr01tjw/pubs/win10-winds.pdf.

28. Palmer, Roy. *The Oxford Book of Sea Songs*. Oxford: Oxford University Press, 1986.

29. A knot is a nautical mile an hour. The term nautical miles and sea miles are used interchangeably. Technically a sea mile is the distance subtended at the Earth's surface by a minute of arc along any meridian – and because the Earth is not a perfect sphere it is shorter on the equator than in the high latitudes. By international agreement a nautical mile is an average sea mile, or about 1.15 land miles. For practical purposes in navigation nautical miles can be easily measured with dividers off the latitude scale at the side of the chart.

Chapter Five

30. Midgley, Mary. 'Philosophical Plumbing.' In *The Essential Mary Midgley*, edited by David Midgley. London: Routledge, 2005, p. 146.

31. Kipling, Rudyard. *Just So Stories*. London: Macmillan, 1902.

32. Thomas Kuhn's *Structure of Scientific Revolutions,* which introduced the term 'paradigm', was published in 1962 and was just beginning to have a major influence.

33. http://www.guardian.co.uk/commentisfree/video/2010/dec/27/mary-midgley-myths-selfish-gene

34. Important support and stimulus for this development in the UK came from the New Paradigm Research Group that we established in London in the mid 1970s. Key members included John Heron, John Rowan, Michaela von Britzke and Jo May Prussak.

35. This change was driven by political events and the devastation brought about by religious conflicts as much as by philosophical innovation. See Toulmin, Stephen. *Cosmopolis: The hidden agenda of modernity*. New York: Free Press, 1990.

36. Skolimowski, Henrik. *The Participatory Mind*. London: Arkana, 1994, p. 152.

37. Ladkin, Donna. 'Talking with Trees: Remembering the Language of Home.' *ReVision* 23, no. 4 (2001): 40-43.

Chapter Six

38. Cheney, Jim. 'Truth, Knowledge, and the Wild World.' *Ethics and the Environment* 10, no. 2 (2005): 101-135, p. 116.

39. Chan is the Chinese ancestor of Zen Buddhism. Both emphasize a direct experiential understanding of the world through meditation practice rather than teachings or scriptures.

40. Berry, Thomas. *The Great Work*.

41. Crook, John H. *Hilltops of the Hong Kong Moon*. London: Minerva Press, 1997.

42. Chan Master Shen-Yeng. *Illuminating Silence: The practice of Chinese Zen*. Edited and with commentary by John Crook. London: Watkins Publishing, 2002.

43. John explored Chan practice in Crook, John H. 'Meaning, Purpose and Insight in Western Chan: Practice after Shifu.' *New Chan Forum* 42 (2010): 1-18. Available at http://www. westernchanfellowship.org/ncf+M5148bff4517.html

44. *Albedo* refers to the reflective quality of the planet that reflects solar energy. Clouds and ice have high albedo, oceans and evergreen forests low albedo. Harding, Stephan P. *Animate Earth*. Foxhole, Dartington: Green Books, 2009, p. 77.

Chapter Seven

45. Steinbeck, John. *The Log from the Sea of Cortez*. London: Heinmann, 1958, p. 267.

46. Quoted in Crist, Eileen, and H. Bruce Rinker. 'One Grand Organic Whole.' In *Gaia in Turmoil: Climate Change, Biodepletion, and Earth Ethics in an Age of Crisis*, edited by Eileen Crist and H. Bruce Rinker, 3-20. Cambridge, MA: The MIT Press, 2010.

47. Dawkins, Richard. *The Selfish Gene* (2nd Revised edition). Oxford: Oxford Paperbacks, 1989.

48. Margulis, Lynn, Celeste A Asikainen, and Wolfgang E Krumbein, eds. *Chimeras and Consciousness: Evolution of the Sensory Self*. Cambridge, MA: The MIT Press, 2011, p. 11.

49. Ward, Peter, and Donald E Brownlee. *Rare Earth: Why Complex Life Is Uncommon in the Universe*. New York: Springer, 2000.

50. Crist, Eileen, and H. Bruce Rinker, eds. *Gaia in Turmoil*, p. 4.

51. Kump, Lee R, James F Kasting, and Robert G Crane. *The Earth System*. 2nd edition. Upper Saddle River, NJ: Prentice-Hall, 2004.

52. Harding, Stephan P. *Animate Earth*, p. 19-29. This strand of pan-psychic philosophy is formally traced by David Skrbina in *Panpsychism in the West*. Cambridge, Mass: MIT Press, 2005.

53. Steinbeck, John. *The Log from the Sea of Cortez*.

Chapter Eight

54. Snyder, Gary. *The Practice of the Wild*, pp. 98-99.

55. Margulis, Lynn, Celeste A Asikainen, and Wolfgang E Krumbein, eds. *Chimeras and Consciousness: Evolution of the Sensory Self*. Cambridge, MA: The MIT Press, 2011, p. 11.

56. Harding, Stephan P, and Lynn Margulis. 'Water Gaia: 3.5 Thousand Million Years of Wetness on Planet Earth.' In *Gaia in Turmoil: Climate Change, Biodepletion, and Earth Ethics in an Age of Crisis*, edited by Eileen Crist and H. Bruce Rinker, 41-59. Cambridge, MA: The MIT Press, 2010.

57. As I understand it, this statement conforms to the current scientific consensus. However, recent research argues that the impact of the North Atlantic Drift on the climate of maritime Europe is actually minimal. An overview of this research can be found in an article in American Scientist at http://www.americanscientist.org/issues/pub/the-source-of-europes-mild-climate that includes references to the original papers.

58. Lavery, Trish J, Ben Roudnew, Peter Gill, Justin Seymour, Laurent Seuront, Genevieve Johnson, James G Mitchell, and Victor Smetacek. 'Iron Defecation by Sperm Whales Stimulates Carbon Export in the Southern Ocean.' *Proceedings of the Royal Society B* 277, no. 1699 (2010): 3527-3531.

59. Flannery, Tim. *Here on Earth*.

60. Snyder, Gary. *The Practice of the Wild*, 1990, p. 82, original emphasis.

61. Snyder, Gary. *The Gary Snyder Reader*, p. 201.

62. Belloc, Hillaire. 'The Idea of Pilgrimage,' in *Hills and the Sea*, 1906. Available at http://www.readbookonline.net/readOnLine/23259/

Chapter Nine
63. Carse, James P. *Finite and Infinite Games: A Vision of Life as Play and Possibility.* Harmondsworth: Penguin, 1987, pp. 3-18.
64. Fortey, Richard. *The Hidden Landscape: A Journey into the Geological Past.* 2nd edition. London: The Bodley Head, 2010.
65. Cunliffe, Barry. *Facing the Ocean: The Atlantic and Its Peoples 8000BC-AD1500.* Oxford: Oxford University Press, 2001.

Chapter Ten
66. Meadows, Donella H. 'Change Is Not Doom.' *ReVision* 14, no. 2 (1991): pp. 56-60.
67. Meadows, Donella, H, Dennis L. Meadows, Jørgen Randers, and William W. Behrens. *The Limits to Growth.* New York: Universe Books, 1972. The book was revised and updated, demonstrating that the original arguments held good, as Meadows, Donella, H, Dennis L. Meadows, Jørgen Randers, and William W. Behrens. *Limits to Growth: The 30-Year Update.* White River Junction, Vt: Chelsea Green, 2004.
68. Meadows, Donella H. 'Change Is Not Doom.'
69. This challenge of exponential growth as a contribution of environmental crisis is explored in *Limits to Growth: The 30-year update.*

Chapter Eleven
70. Chang Tsai, eleventh century Confucian philosopher. Quoted in Tu, Wei-Ming. "The Continuity of Being". In J. B. Callicott & R. T. Ames eds. *Nature in Asian Traditions of Thought.* Albany: SUNY Press, 1989, pp. 73-74.
71. Berry, Thomas. *The Great Work.*
72. From an interview in 2001 republished in *Enlightenment Magazine* http://www.enlightennext.org/magazine/j34/swimme1.asp?page=2. I am grateful to Helena Kettleborough for alerting me to this quote.
73. For thorough (and rather different) expositions of panpsychic philosophy see Mathews, Freya. *For Love of Matter: A Contemporary Panpsychism.* Albany, NY: SUNY Press, 2003; and Strawson, Galen, and et al. *Consciousness and Its Place in Nature: Does Physicalism Entail Panpsychism?* Exeter: Imprint Academic, 2006. For a historical account see Skrbina, David. *Panpsychism in the West.* Cambridge, Mass: MIT Press, 2005.
74. Matthiessen, Peter. *The Snow Leopard.* London: Picador, 1980, p. 225.

Chapter Twelve
75. Synge, J.M. *Travels in Wicklow, West Kerry, and Connemara.* London: Serif, 2005 (1911).
76. There are three autobiographical books written originally in Gaelic by people who lived there and two by visitors who developed a deep familiarity with island life: O'Sullivan, Maurice. *Twenty Years a-Growing* (First Published 1933). Translated by Moya Llewelyn Davies and George Thomson. Oxford: Oxford University Press, 1953; Ó Crohan, Tomás. *The Islandman.* Translated by Robin Flower. Dublin: The Talbot Press, 1937; Sayers, Peig. *Peig: The Autobiography of Peig Sayers.* Translated by Bryan MacMahon. Dublin: The Talbot Press, 1974; Singles, Joan, and Ray Singles. *The Blasket Islands: Next Parish America.* Dublin: O'Brian Press, 1984; Flower, Robin. *The Western Island.* Oxford: Clarendon Press, 1944.
77. Snyder, Gary. The *Practice of the Wild.* p. 94-96.
78. Crook, John H. *The Koans of Layman John:* Available from the Western Chan Fellowship

www.westernchanfellowship.org, 2009.

79. Macfarlane, Robert. 'A Counter-Desecration Handbook.' In *Towards Re-Enchantment: Place and Its Meanings,* edited by Gareth Evans and Di Robson. London: Artevents, 2010.

80. An introduction to the mind of the dolphin with Peter Russell and Duane Elgin is available at http://www.peteandduane.com/home/mind-of-the-dolphin/

Chapter Thirteen

81. Julian of Norwich, (c1413) Revelations of Divine Love. As rendered by Fox, Matthew. *Original Blessing: A Primer in Creation Spirituality.* Santa Fe, NM: Bear & Company, Inc., 1983, p. 43.

82. Tim O'Shea (nd) *The Skelligs.* See also http://www.prayerfoundation.org/skellig_michael_monastery.htm

83. Hillman, James. *Revisioning Psychology.* New York: Harper Collophon, 1975, p. x.

84. Kumar, Satish. *Earth Pilgrim: Conversations with Satish Kumar.* Dartington: Green Books, 2009. The BBC2 Natural World Documentary with Satish Kumar available at http://www.youtube.com/watch?v=6de9FjR40g0

85. This is Ursula Le Guin's version. She notes that a satisfactory rendering of this verse is 'perfectly impossible'. Le Guin, Ursula. *Lao Tzu: Tao Te Ching.* Boston, MA: Shambhala, 1997, p. 3.

86. Cunliffe, Barry. *Facing the Ocean,* pp. 11-12.

87. Recent scholarship by Douglas Christie shows this clearly. Douglas E Christie, *The Blue Sapphire of the Mind: Notes for a contemplative ecology.* New York: Oxford University Press, 2013. Reason, Peter. 'Review, the Blue Sapphire of the Mind: Notes for a Contemplative Ecology by Douglas E Christie.' *Resurgence & Ecologist* no. 281 November/December (2013): 60-61.

88. Moorhouse, Geoffrey. *Sun Dancing.* London: Phoenix, 1997.

89. For quotes and discussion see Fox, Matthew. *Original Blessing: A primer in creation spirituality.* pp. 35-59.

Chapter Fourteen

90. Snyder, Gary. (1990). "The Etiquette of Freedom". In *The Practice of the Wild,* pp. 11-12, emphasis in original.

91. *The Guardian,* Friday 3 June 2011, Geologists press for recognition of Earth-changing 'human epoch.' http://www.guardian.co.uk/science/2011/jun/03/geologists-human-epoch-anthropocene?INTCMP=SRCH

92. McKibben, Bill. *The End of Nature: Humanity, Climate Change and the Natural World.* Revised and updated edition. London: Bloomsbury, 2003.

93. Berry, Thomas. *The Great Work,* p. 8.

94. Flannery, Tim. *Here on Earth.*

95. This is the argument well made in the Club of Rome's *Limits to Growth,* in 1972 one of the earliest books to challenge orthodox assumptions about economic growth. The second edition of the book was actually titled *Beyond the Limits.*

96. *The Daily Telegraph* 31 Aug 2010. Retrieved from http://www.telegraph.co.uk/sport/othersports/sailing/7966301/Ellen-MacArthur-I-cant-live-with-the-sea-any-more.html January 1 2011.

97. Berry, Thomas. *The Great Work,* p. 50.

98. Macfarlane, Robert. *Mountains of the Mind: A History of a Fascination.* London: Granta Books, 2004, p. 74.

99. Thoreau, Henry David. 'Walking.' *Atlantic Monthly.* (1862) *(Available at http://thoreau.*

eserver.org/walking.html).

100. Lopez, Barry Holstun. *Of Wolves and Men*. London: John Dent and Sons, 1978, p. 140.

101. Thoreau, Henry David. "Walking".

102. Griffiths, Jay. *Wild: An Elemental Journey*. London: Hamish Hamilton, 2006, p. 2, emphasis in original.

103. Bateson, Gregory. *Steps to an Ecology of Mind*, 1972.

104. Berry, Thomas. *The Great Work*, pp. 48-50.

105. Flannery, Tim. *Here on Earth*.

106. Snyder, Gary. *The Practice of the Wild*, p. 127.

107. Maughan, Esther, and Peter Reason. 'A Co-Operative Inquiry into Deep Ecology.' *ReVision* 23, no. 4 (2001): 18-24. Reprinted as Maughan McLachlan, Esther, and Peter Reason. 'A Co-Operative Inquiry into Deep Ecology.' In *Grow Small, Think Beautiful: Ideas for a Sustainable World from Schumacher College*, edited by Stephan Harding. Edinbugh: Floris Books, 2011.

108. Bate, Jonathan. *The Song of the Earth*. London: Picador, 2000, p. 143.

109. Quoted in Lafargue, Michael. '"Nature" As Part of Human Culture in Daoism.' In *Daoism and Ecology: Ways within a Cosmic Landscape*, edited by N.J. Girardot, James Miller and Liu Xiaogan, 45-59. Cambridge, MA: Harvard University Press, 2001, p. 47.

Chapter Fifteen

110. Abram, David. *The Spell of the Sensuous*, p. ix.

111. See Mathews, Freya. *For Love of Matter*.

112. Abram, David. *The Spell of the Sensuous*, p. ix.

Chapter Sixteen

113. Swimme, Brian Thomas, and Mary Evelyn Tucker. *The Journey of the Universe*. New Haven: Yale University Press, 2011, pp. 1-2. See also DVD, *The Journey of the Universe: An Epic Story of Cosmic, Earth, and Human Transformation* available at www.journeyoftheuniverse.org

114. Dellinger, Drew. *Love Letter to the Milky Way*. Mill Valley, CA: Planetize the Movement Press, 2010.

115. Swimme, Brian, and Thomas Berry. *The Universe Story: From the Primordial Flaring Forth to the Ecozoic Era--a Celebration of the Unfolding of the Cosmos*. New York: HarperCollins, 1992. See also Swimme, Brian Thomas, and Mary Evelyn Tucker. *The Journey of the Universe*.

116. Flannery, Tim. *Here on Earth*.

117. Aquinas, Thomas. *Summa Contra Gentiles*. Translated by Anton C. Pegis. Notre Dame, IN: University of Notre Dame Press, 1955.

118. Berry, Thomas. *The Great Work*, p. 107.

Chapter Seventeen

119. Nietzsche, Friedrich. 'Schopenhauer as Educator.' In *The Untimely Meditations (Thoughts out of Season Part II)*, trans Adrian Collins, 1874.

120. Rilke, Rainer Maria. *Letters to a Young Poet*. Translated by Stephen Mitchell. Modern Library Classics. New York: Random House, 1984.

121. Snyder, Gary. *The Practice of the Wild*, p. 94.

122. Crook, John H. *The Koans of Layman John*.

123. Rilke, Rainer Maria. *Turning Point: Miscellaneous Poems 1912-1926* Translated by Michael Hamburger. London: Anvil Press Poetry, 2003, p. 51.

About Vala

Vala is an adventure
in community supported publishing.

We are a co-operative
bringing books to the world that explore and celebrate
the human spirit with brave and authentic
ways of thinking and being.

Books that seek to help us find our own meanings
that may lead us in new and unexpected directions.

Vala's co-operative members
- suggest authors
- design
- write
- support the writing process
- get together for book-making evenings
- promote and sell Vala books through their own networks.

Members come together to celebrate and launch each
new publication. Together we decide what happens to any
profit that we make.

Vala exists to bring us all into fuller relationship with our
world, ourselves, and each other.

To find out more visit us at *www.valapublishers.coop*